THE
FRE

A comprehensiv ... .. most of a
deep-freeze, prov ... un freezing, thawing
and storage life .. a range of wholefoods and
vegetarian recipes.

By the same author:
VEGETARIAN COOKER-TOP COOKERY

THE WHOLEFOOD FREEZER BOOK

The First Freezer Book for Wholefooders and Vegetarians

by

PAMELA BROWN

Illustrated by Clive Birch

THORSONS PUBLISHERS LIMITED
Wellingborough, Northamptonshire

First published 1980
Second Impression 1982

British Library Cataloguing in Publication Data

Brown, Pamela
  The wholefood freezer book.
  1. Vegetarian cookery
  2. Food, Frozen
  I. Title
  641.5'55   TX837

  ISBN 0-7225-0619-8
  ISBN 0-7225-0588-4 Pbk

Printed in Great Britain by
King's English Bookprinters Limited, Bramley, Leeds
and bound by Weatherby Woolnough, Wellingborough,
Northamptonshire.

CONTENTS

		Page
Introduction		7
Chapter		
1.	Managing the Freezer	11
2.	Freezer Foods	19
3.	Freezing Vegetables and Fruit	25
4.	Pastry	39
5.	Cheese	44
6.	Eggs	54
7.	Vegetables	56
8.	Soya Protein	67
9.	Beans and Pulses	73
10.	Nuts	84
11.	Rice and Wholegrains	92
12.	Pancakes and Pasta	99
13.	Sauces and Soups	106
14.	Bread, Scones, Biscuits and Cakes	115
15.	Sweet Dishes	126
16.	Quick Meals from the Freezer	137
17.	Entertaining With Your Freezer	146
18.	Sandwiches	152
19.	Fresh Raw Foods	156
	Recipe Index	159

DEDICATION

I would like to dedicate this book to all the mothers who find themselves faced with a child saying, 'I don't want to eat meat'. I hope my efforts will help them cope with their vegetarian children and continue to have a healthy, happy family.

INTRODUCTION

This book is written in response to the innumerable requests that I have received for information about freezing wholefoods and vegetarian dishes.

There are many freezer books on the market with plenty of information about the straightforward use of the freezer, but none that I know include the answers to the questions I am so often asked. For example, 'Can I freeze wholegrains?', 'Will 100 per cent wholewheat flour spoil?', 'What happens to lentils?', 'How about freezing nuts?'

All the answers are here. The recipes are designed for use with wholefoods, that is, unrefined grains, rice, pulses, flour and pasta. This is a vegetarian cook book, with lots of recipes combining vegetables with wholefoods, herbs and spices to give delicious meals that taste and look good. Milk, cheese and eggs are used, but in moderation. Those recipes which need not include animal produce are marked with an asterisk.

Anyone unfamiliar with a vegetarian diet need have no fears that they will suffer nutritionally. Nuts and dairy produce will provide all the protein needed. Wholegrains, pulses etc. and vegetables and fruit will not only provide necessary vitamins and minerals but protein as well. I am reminded of the words of a specialist in gastro-intestinal problems when we were appearing together on an Ulster Television programme. He said, 'Many of my friends are vegetarians, but none of my patients!'

The recipe section of this book can be used as an ordinary cookery book. Each recipe is clearly explained right through to serving. After that, advice is given about how to prepare the dish for the freezer, the length of storage time and how to thaw and serve.

Charts show the best way of freezing fruit and vegetables. There is advice about freezing dairy produce, baked goods, sauces, sandwiches, soups, cooked savouries and sweets.

People living alone often ask for my advice, and I suggest

that they buy a freezer. There is a chapter here showing how life can be changed and eating become more economical for the lone freezer owner.

Suggestions are given for entertaining the easy way, most of the work being done in advance! There are ideas for special decorative touches that cost little in time or money. Children's parties are seen in a new light because you can have most of the food prepared well in advance leaving time to concentrate on the games. You will have enough energy to actually enjoy it because you are not exhausted with food preparation on the day.

The same goes for all other entertaining – even picnics, because there is a special sandwich section, and ideas for something that is different to eat 'al fresco'.

Which Freezer?

Having decided that you would benefit by owning a freezer you have to determine which type, how big, and where to put it. Before buying it is sensible to read a lot of literature, look around the shops and talk to freezer owning friends. There are many regular freezer books that give detailed information about choice and management.

Although my main purpose in this book is to give information about wholefoods for the freezer, and not to go into all the pros and cons of freezer management, I am sure the following basic points will be of help in choosing and maintaining your freezer to the best advantage.

First decide on the best location for your circumstances. Ideally this should be a dry, airy and cool place. The kitchen is the most convenient, but it should not be near the cooker and it must have air round about it. Since you will not be opening the freezer very often a cool utility room, porch or even garage are possible sites. (But do not put it too far from the kitchen or you may find you do not make full use of it!)

Size is important, and on the whole it is better to buy a large freezer. Around 3 cubic feet per person is generally thought reasonable. Chest models are more economical to run since the cold air does not escape as quickly as it does when an upright model is opened. But a small person may find a chest model more difficult to negotiate. You must experiment in the shop to be sure that you can easily reach down to the far corner!

There is also a tendency for food to 'get lost' in a chest model, so management is important. (See page 11) Upright models take up less floor space, and there are quite small ones that stand on top of an existing refrigerator. Indeed, you could buy a freezer-fridge combination. On the whole a larger freezer will cost less in comparison, but one must also consider the amount of electricity that will be used.

BRITISH/AMERICAN EQUIVALENTS

Liquid Measure Equivalents

British	American
1 teaspoonful	1¼ teaspoonsful
1 tablespoonful	1¼ tablespoonsful
1 pint (20 fl oz)	1¼ pints

Cup Measures

A British standard measuring cup contains 10 fl oz (275ml).
An American standard measuring cup contains 8 fl oz (225ml).

Note: Where margarine is included in recipes it is understood that this means vegetable margarine.

1
MANAGING
THE FREEZER

Your freezer must be used to give maximum return. This means a well thought out management plan. You will have chosen the size and type of freezer according to your life-style and environment and now you must work out how best to use it.

Plan to use the least accessible areas for long term storage – once a year items like fruit and vegetables mostly. If there are baskets, choose the nearest one to your work surface for all the small items that will be in your freezer to save time and money; for example, cubes of tomato *purée*, bags of herbs, sauces, roux, eggs. Any other baskets should be allocated types of produce as with baked goods and savouries.

You are wasting time and money if you leave things in the deep freeze too long and they become spoiled, so you must know what is there. The best way is to keep lists (although I must admit that I find it very difficult to keep a record up to date).

Some Suggestions

Lists are ideal and for some people essential. Whether you keep them up to date or not you must work to some order in the deep freeze and this can be achieved in several ways. Here are some suggestions:

Containers
To keep things as cold as possible you must have the freezer reasonably full and not have lots of spaces. Use square containers as much as possible. Liquids can be frozen in a polythene bag within a square box which can later be removed.

Labelling
Colour code labels are essential. After the first flush of enthusiastic labelling it is very easy to pop something in unlabelled being absolutely sure that you will recognize it

again. But several months later you will find that puréed soup can look very like apple snow – a tragedy in the making! If you do not have them already, when you next go shopping buy a variety of coloured labels and decide which colours to use for each type of food.

A further refinement when labelling is to identify each month with a coloured sticker. Buy a variety of tiny labels in different colours and shapes, then work out your key for the year. For instance one could use a green circle for January an orange star for February yellow square for March and so on. This means you can at a glance calculate how long food has been in the freezer. It is also best to write the date before which food should be eaten. Keep your key chart near the freezer for quick reference. Obviously there are many ways of managing the date problem, the above is an idea for you to work on and come up with something that suits you.

Allocating Freezer Space

You need to allocate areas in the freezer for different types of food. Baskets are easy, but, particularly in the chest type of freezer there are wide spaces in which packages can easily become lost. After trying different things, such as cardboard boxes etc., I have settled for using plastic shopping bags. Mine are the big 'Humane Research Trust' carriers that are available in five different colours. They are cheap, and easily replaced. I keep all the bread and rolls in an orange one and apple *purées* in green and so on. This keeps the freezer tidy and gives space for odds and ends in between.

What Containers to Use

When you have planned your system and space allocation you can think about essential storage items. These do not need to be expensive. You need plenty of good quality polythene bags and they can often be washed and re-used. See-through bags help identification of contents.

Square plastic containers can be used as 'freezer formers'. Put a polythene bag into the container, fill with liquid or *purée* and then freeze. Remove the container and you have a flat square shape, easy to store and quicker to thaw than an irregular lump.

Plastic containers from bought items such as margarine or yogurt will always be useful. A few waxed tubs and cartons are handy, but be sure never to put hot liquid in these or you will have food with a high wax content!

Tins can also be used, especially those with tight fitting lids. Round tins of course are less economical of space than square ones. Whichever you use you must be sure that you have excluded as much air as possible and that the lid is secure.

Glass jars are useful for juice, but again are rather wasteful of space. To be sure they will stand the temperature you can test by putting an empty jar in a plastic bag in the freezer for a few days. If it does break you have no problems about collecting the glass.

Aluminium foil dishes are obtainable in every shape and size. They are time saving, but expensive and unattractive for serving food. A big roll of foil lasts a long time and means that you can use your ordinary dishes by lining them, freezing and then removing the dish.

Some people prefer not to use foil in any way and for them a great asset are the dishes that are guaranteed safe when taken from the freezer and put straight into a hot oven. (A spin-off from the space programme.) Essential items are wire closures, a felt tip pen for writing on plastic tubs etc. and perhaps some freezer tape (ordinary sticky tape is no use).

Packaging

Always remember that liquids and *purées* expand when frozen and so you must leave enough head room. With other foods the aim is to exclude as much air as possible. Make sure the polythene bags are air tight, pack your food in and then draw out air – you can suck it out through a drinking straw. Twist the top and fix with a wire closure.

If space has to be left in a container (for some delicate sort of food) fill the space with crumpled tissue paper to keep as much air as possible from the food.

Freezing is one of the best ways of storing food – but only if it is well packaged. When food is exposed to air in the freezer it becomes dehydrated, dry and uninteresting. Oxygen in the air reacts with fat cells to form chemicals which can produce bad tastes.

Your Health and Your Freezer

It has been established that quick freezing of food is the best method of preservation. The action of enzymes and bacteria is halted at low temperatures. This is because the water in each tiny cell is frozen. Quick freezing is essential in order to produce the smallest possible ice crystals. Slow freezing allows time for these crystals to be larger and they are then forced through the delicate walls of the cells causing damage to the texture and quality of the food.

So long as food is well wrapped, properly frozen and kept at the correct temperature, 0°F or lower, it will remain in good condition for long periods and be absolutely safe to eat. In fact, less food value will be lost than with other forms of preservation such as canning and the use of artificial preservatives.

This is obviously not to say that all one's food can be eaten from the deep freeze. Food that would normally be cooked loses very little food value by being frozen, but food to be eaten raw will not normally go into the freezer – except for a few fruits such as raspberries, citrus fruits, melons and grapes.

For good health it is essential to eat some raw food each day, and this is outside the scope of this book. Because raw food is so essential a short section of the book is, however, devoted to the preparation of raw vegetables and the growing of sprouted seeds, both of which can be used as an accompaniment to main dishes.

One of the many advantages of owning a freezer is the way in which one can freeze fruit without sugar, this can eliminate the use of canned fruits which are invariably soaked in heavy syrup. Another advantage is being able to have what are virtually fresh herbs, with their health-giving properties all year round.

Will it be Cheaper?

The economics of running a freezer vary with each individual user. There is no doubt that life becomes less complicated because you need to shop less often. That means you can bulk buy which is certainly cheaper.

Vegetarians already have an advantage over meat eaters in this respect because they can buy in large quantities grains, beans, pulses etc. which do not deteriorate and which form a major part of their diet. Even though nuts do not keep long in ordinary storage they can be kept very well in a freezer.

The most obvious benefit is when you grow your own food and all the surplus goes into the freezer (instead of being given away to friends!) Further, when fruit and vegetables are at their peak they can be bought in bulk, or even picked yourself to obtain the cheapest price. There can also be a saving on fuel when you bake extra items at one time, some of which are destined for the freezer.

Great satisfaction comes in making good use of left-overs and if these go into the freezer carefully packed and labelled they can appear later as an unremembered meal. Another saving is almost hidden. In busy lives most of us tend to leave things to the last minute, and this may well result in an eleventh hour dash to the shops to buy expensive ready made food. With a freezer you cut this out. Having made these items when you had time you simply have to make your choice.

You do of course have to remember in advance that you want to thaw something out. It is a good idea to have a special place in the freezer for quick thawing items. Suggestions for quick meals from the freezer can be found on page 137.

Storage Times

Storage times can only be very approximate as so much depends on the following variables:

The quality of the food when frozen. The freezer does not improve quality and so if food is not first rate when it goes in it certainly will not be wonderful when it comes out.

Wrapping. If the wrapping is not as air free as possible oxygen in the air will get to work on the food and it will deteriorate. So you must wrap really well and check on wrappings from time to time.

Speed of freezing. This is very important, as has been explained on page 13. If the food is not fast frozen, or is still warm when put in the freezer the formation of larger crystals will affect the quality.

The temperature in the freezer. If it is allowed to rise – by leaving unswitched for some time, or having the door open too much – again the quality of food will be impaired.

Approximate storage times are given for all recipes. These tend to be on the short side, almost certainly food will be perfectly alright if left quite a bit longer. However, it is best to try to work roughly within these times until your own experience tells you differently.

How to Thaw

Much is said about the necessity to defrost and cook food right through. But there are not the same dangers about defrosting and cooking meatless dishes as in animal foods. Obviously it is necessary to heat cooked food right through. Nothing is worse than being served an appetizing dish only to take a mouthful of tasteless ice!

For this reason it is often better to allow dishes to thaw

completely before reheating. A slow thaw in the fridge is preferable. Where, in what follows, it is suggested to thaw overnight in the fridge it is assumed that the dish will not be cooked until well into the next day. This requires good planning and foreknowledge of the next day's requirements.

If the freezer is to be a solution to the problem of sudden demands for food there must, of course, be quick ways to thaw. Unwrapped at room temperature most baked goods will thaw within the hour. Bread, scones and cakes can be put in a slow oven for quick defrosting, but should then be used up quickly.

Running warm water over the container will start thawing soups, sauces and casseroles; then they can be transferred to a saucepan and heated, very gently until there is some liquid in the bottom. As the outside softens the food can be carefully broken up with a fork and completely heated.

A hair dryer can even be brought into play on extreme occasions!

It is impossible to give exact times for thawing since several factors come in, including warmth of the environment and actual thickness of the food. Suggested thawing times for each recipe must be taken as a guide line. The main thing is to give more time, rather than less.

Cooking for One

People living alone frequently lack the incentive to make interesting meals. They often ask me for recipes with only enough for one person. 'How can I adapt ordinary recipes for four?' is the frequent query. Surprisingly this is not easy. How do you judge a quarter of an egg or a quarter of a pinch of salt? In any case it hardly seems worth lighting an oven to cook small amounts for one meal – and no one wants to eat the same thing for three or four days in order to use it up! Consequently single people tend not to bother and manage with bought bread and cakes, cheese, eggs and maybe some salad.

Yet the answer is so obvious – buy a small freezer. It opens up a whole new way of eating, will be economical and provide endless variety. The best choice may well be a combined fridge-freezer. But be careful; think about just how useful the freezer will be, and do not buy one that is too small.

There will be no longer any need to try to prepare single portions all the time. Generally recipes are for four and most cooked dishes will keep perfectly in the freezer for 2 to 3 months. In fact if well packed they will usually be quite all right for longer.

So with an average 10 main meals a week – in three months 120 meals – you will be able to provide yourself with a great variety and some lovely 'cook-in' days. The best possible use can be made of the oven and when dishes have been allowed to cool they can be divided into suitable portions and frozen separately. Whole menus can be packed together – soup, savoury and sweet – ringing the changes with a different sauce.

Another advantage of owning a freezer is the facility of being able to prepare recipes when the oven is not in use and freezing them uncooked. For instance you could prepare a nut savoury. Use some of it for burgers that day and put the rest in the freezer all ready in a loaf tin for baking later. On the day that you bake the nut savoury you can eat what you need, then slice the rest and freeze to use another time.

Using your freezer this way all the recipes in this book are available to you. In fact you can now open any recipe book with a feeling of adventure – instead of despair.

Shopping will become easier and cheaper – you can buy in larger quantities and greater variety. You will also conserve your energy. If you are elderly this is especially important. You can do things when you feel up to it, and reap the benefits on days when life seems more of an effort!

Although of course if you are following the recipes in this book and living on a good wholefood diet with lots of raw fruit and vegetables you will probably have boundless energy.

One last piece of special advice to you if you live alone. Try to divide your portions very neatly and wherever possible bake individual pies and little dishes, while still using the recipe for four people. Prepared like this the food will look more appetizing and will not appear as left-overs.

One in the Family

All that I have said for the single person applies to the lone vegetarian in a family. Try to annex a portion of the freezer for yourself (I mean your food!). In no time you will have the rest of the family wanting to try your dishes when they see how very interesting they can be.

Mothers of children who refuse to eat meat will also find using a freezer in this way invaluable. I particularly hope this book will help mothers in this position because I am faced so often with a distraught mother who is uncertain how to be sure that her child is getting the right nutrition without eating meat, and who does not always have time to make different meals for one member of the family.

2
FREEZER FOODS

Dairy Produce

Milk. Although there seems little point in freezing milk it is possible to do so. Homogenized milk freezes best. Put it into a wax carton or polythene bag in a suitable container which can be removed when milk is frozen and remember to allow enough head room.

Cheese. Some cheeses, such as cheddar, crumble after freezing, but the taste is still good. Ripe soft cheeses, such as camembert, are unaffected. Allow cheese to thaw and warm up before eating. Grated cheese can be stored in polythene bags in the freezer for immediate use in hot dishes – or for speedy thawing if to be used on salads etc. Cottage cheese can be frozen for up to 4 months, others up to 6 months.

Cream. Cream freezes well if there is a high fat content. It is very useful for decorating if frozen in rosettes. Open freeze and then pack carefully. It is excellent for whipping after being frozen (but not much good in coffee!). It can be frozen for up to 6 months. However, if it is whipped it cannot be frozen as long.

Eggs. They must be beaten up before freezing. They can be frozen with yolks and whites beaten together or separately. The addition of a little salt or sugar helps the texture. Freeze in small containers, labelling the number of eggs in each pack and whether they are sweet or savoury. Thaw eggs by standing in room temperature for about 40 minutes.

  3 tablespoonsful = 1 whole egg
  2 tablespoonsful = 1 egg white
  1 tablespoonful = 1 yolk

Egg whites whip very well after freezing. Eggs can be frozen for 8-10 months.

Bread, Biscuits and Cakes
Cooked bread, biscuits and cakes keep extremely well in the freezer. In fact I sometimes think their texture is actually improved by freezing.

Families accustomed to home-made bread need never be forced to fall back on the shop variety when the bread bin is bare! It is almost as easy to make a double batch at one time, and this makes good use of the oven.

Allow bread to cool completely before freezing. Some people advise freezing one day old bread. It is a good idea to cut a few slices, slipping a piece of foil or film between them. Freeze these with the loaf in a polythene bag; you can use the slices straight out of the freezer for toast, or if you left it a bit late, remembering you needed bread from the freezer, the separate slices will thaw very quickly.

Bread can be frozen for as long as 8 months. It must be well wrapped for that time, although, if needed within a week or two, only light wrapping is necessary. It should be thawed in the wrapping at room temperature for about 3 hours. To thaw quickly unwrap and put in a moderate oven. Bread thawed like this needs to be used quickly.

Raw bread dough can be frozen, although the result may be less than perfect. However, it is good to know that in an emergency you can put risen dough into the freezer. Freeze in the tin, then remove and wrap when the dough is frozen. Store for only 2-3 weeks. Return to the original tin and thaw in a very warm place, such as an airing cupboard, and make sure the bread is properly risen before baking.

Fresh yeast can be frozen for a short time – not more than 2 months. To use, put it in to a small bowl in a very warm place, sprinkle a little soft brown sugar or molasses over and just cover with very warm water. In a few minutes you will be able to cream the yeast, then add more water and stir well. (For bread recipes turn to page 115.)

It is useful to have some cakes and scones in the freezer. You can use 100 per cent or 81 per cent flour and vegetarian margarines, and nut fats or vegetarian oils. When making cakes for the freezer bear in mind that artificial flavours tend to change, so it is better to use sugar in which vanilla pods have been stored, fresh lemon, etc. rather than artificial essences. Mix eggs well as yolk and white freeze slightly differently and this may spoil the texture. Spices can develop off flavours and so storage times should be shorter for any food that is well spiced.

On the whole it is better not to decorate cakes before freezing. White sugar icing tends to go soggy. Since it is better to avoid white sugar anyway other decorations are to be preferred. A simple brown sugar butter icing freezes very well. Another nutritious topping is a smear of honey covered by chopped nuts, and this can be frozen.

Cakes and scones can be stored for 3-4 months. They should be thawed at room temperature, in their wrappings if possible. The time will depend on their size and how warm the place is, but cakes generally thaw very quickly. Small sponges can almost be eaten right away! If they need to be thawed in a hurry take them out of their wrappings and put in a very warm place.

Uncooked cake mixtures can be frozen (not fatless sponge mixtures). The best way is to line baking tins with foil, open freeze, then remove and wrap. To use the cake mixture unwrap it and return to the well greased tin. Put straight into a pre-heated oven, baked at the normal temperature, allowing extra time.

Biscuit doughs are worth freezing shaped in a roll. This can be thinly cut while still frozen and immediately baked. Sections can be round, square, triangular, oval, oblong and different flavours can be rolled together (such as chocolate and vanilla) to give great variety. The dough can be stored for up to 2 months.

Cooked Savouries

All cooked savouries can be frozen. Storage times will depend on the ingredients, for instance garlic, onion and strong spices tend to be affected by the cold and develop off flavours. Dishes with these flavours should only be stored for a short time. Fat can also be affected, and dishes with a high fat content will not be so good if stored for a long time. This does not mean that they will be harmful to eat, but that the taste may be impaired.

When freezing cooked savouries it is important to see that they are cooled as quickly as possible and only frozen when cold. It is better to undercook slightly as they will have to be thoroughly heated and therefore cooked a bit more. It is difficult to give exact timings for reheating as there are so many variables.

With vegetarian dishes there is not the same danger of food poisoning by eating partially cooked meat, but of course it is essential to have the inside of the dish really hot, and so a check must be made some time before serving.

Most savouries can be frozen uncooked. This makes it possible to prepare dishes when the oven is not in use. Put straight from frozen into the oven when they are to be eaten. Care must be taken in choosing a suitable container that will not be harmed by taking from freezer to oven. There is a lot to be said for freezing uncooked foods, but extra time must be given to allow it to cook right through. Also, it may be necessary to cover the top with a piece of foil toward the end of the cooking time to avoid burning.

Cooked Puddings

The foregoing applies to most cooked sweet dishes such as sponge puddings and crumbles. (For pies see notes about pastry.) These dishes all freeze well cooked, but if they are to be eaten hot it is probably better to freeze raw and do the entire cooking when needed. They will store in the freezer for about 2 months. Make these puddings in the usual way. Place in a container suitable for freezing and cooking, or line the basin with foil, open freeze and then remove the basin and wrap the food. These puddings can go straight from freezer to oven or steamer. See recipe section for individual instructions.

Crumble mixtures can be stored already prepared in the freezer in a polythene bag. This will remain crumbly and can be used straight on fruit for immediate cooking.

Fresh fruit salads can be stored in a very light syrup or a thin agar jelly with a little lemon juice to retard discoloration. Such salads are better prepared and eaten straight away, but there may be times when it is necessary to prepare well in advance or when left-overs need to be stored. They can be kept for several months.

Mousses and cold soufflés made with agar freeze well, but should only be stored for about 1 month. Remove 2-3 hours before needed depending on the room temperature. They should be served very cold.

Ice-creams made with fresh fruit will stay good for many months in the freezer, as will sorbets. Moulds made in elaborate shapes can be frozen in the shaped container and released perfectly by dipping into hot water for 1 second only. They can then be returned to the freezer until 1 hour before serving.

Pastry

Pastry can be frozen raw or cooked. The only exception is chou pastry which has to be cooked.

For me there is sometimes a certain luxury in being able to make pastry and prepare pies, tarts and so on, and then put them straight into the freezer instead of being tied to the oven until they are all cooked. There is also the advantage of being able to freeze extra uncooked pies when baking some of them. Indeed when you run out of time the uncooked ones can go into the freezer.

Pastry goods from the freezer can be put straight into a hot oven allowing extra time for cooking. Remember it may be a good idea to cover the top with foil towards the end of the time.

Pastry can also be frozen in a block before shaping. It is best to roll it into a thinnish oblong for quick freezing and subsequent thawing. Wrap well and label.

Pastry made with 100 per cent or 81 per cent flour can be stored for up to two months. Allow to thaw at room temperature for about 2 hours. There is a tendency for this kind of pastry to discolour so use it as soon as it is workable, and bake right away.

There are dishes on the market that can be safely kept for some time in a freezer and then put straight into the oven. Special foil dishes are suitable for this. If you have neither you can line the dish with foil, open freeze, and then remove the dish to store the frozen food. When you come to cook simply peel off the foil and put the food onto the original dish. You should, however, allow some thawing to take place before putting into the oven as the extreme cold and heat may crack the dish.

Any pastry food that would normally be brushed over with milk or egg should be left plain for freezing. The wash can be put over the frozen pastry before putting in the oven.

Uncooked fruit pies should not be cut on the top before freezing, the best thing to do is put the pie straight into the oven, and after about 10 minutes slit the top to allow steam to come out.

To prevent soggy bottoms you should brush the pastry with melted butter or margarine before adding the fruit. It is best to open freeze pies and then wrap and label when frozen. Baking on a tin helps to crisp the bottom of pastry.

Chou pastry can be made using 100 per cent flour with the

bran sieved out. It is lighter if 81 per cent flour is used – or even half sieved 100 per cent and half unbleached white flour. Puff pastry is also better with the lighter flours. If made with 100 per cent flour it tastes good but inevitably will not be so light.

Most pastry will store well for up to 2 months – cooked or uncooked. However, it is better not to leave wholewheat goods longer than this.

Ready mixed flour and fat can be kept in a polythene bag in the freezer for about 2 months. This can be used straight from frozen and makes excellent pastry. Store in weighed amounts.

3

FREEZING VEGETABLES AND FRUIT

The charts which follow show accepted methods for freezing fruit and vegetables.

When blanching you must make sure that you have plenty of boiling water. Keep it fast boiling and add a little food at a time, bring quickly back to the boil, and then be sure not to keep the food any longer in the water than the times specified. Special sieves can be bought to enable food to be plunged in and brought out quickly.

When food is removed from the heat it should be cooled as quickly as possible. In most cases this is best done by plunging straight into ice-cold water. Keep changing this water for progressive amounts of food. Dry the food off as much as possible and only freeze when it is really cool.

As far as possible freeze in small quantities, and do not wait for large amounts to accumulate. Put in the freezer at the coldest setting as soon as the food is ready. Put the food to be frozen near the walls, which are coldest, and not near other food.

The times given for blanching assume that shop bought vegetables are used. Freshly picked home grown vegetables are likely to need a much shorter time. It is best to experiment a little before freezing too much. In fact, if you are storing vegetables in the freezer for only a few weeks there is no need to blanch at all. Just clean, prepare, dry and wrap well, label and freeze.

When freezing fruit, I feel it is best, where possible, to avoid using sugar. However, there are a few fruits which keep better in a light sugar syrup which can be made up from 2 cupful of sugar dissolved in 4 cupful of boiling water. When the sugar is dissolved, allow to cool, and then drop fruit – such as apricots – straight into the syrup. Honey can be used instead of sugar, but it will flavour the fruit. Brown sugar accelerates discolouration, while lemon juice in the syrup helps to keep a good colour.

FRUIT	METHOD	STORAGE LIFE	HOW TO THAW
Apples	For maximum saving of space *purée* apples and pack in usable quantities. Peel, core and slice, cook to a *purée* with a little lemon juice in a minimum of water. Cool and freeze. Alternatively, cut out only bruised or bad parts of the apples. Cook in a very little water until apples are quite soft. Put through a *mouli-sieve*, cool and freeze. This preserves all the goodness but is not such a good colour as the first method.	1 yr	Bring from freezer 3 to 4 hours before needed or thaw overnight in fridge.
Apple Juice	Obtain juice by putting through electric juicer or cider press. Strain through muslin. Sterilize by boiling in large saucepan for 1 minute or bringing up to pressure in pressure cooker. Turn off and allow to cool slightly. As soon as cool enough, pour into sterilized bottles, leave expansion space – cover, label and, when cold, freeze. Apples can also be frozen if they are sliced, steeped in lemon juice water, then drained and frozen in usable quantities.	8 to 10 mths 8 mths	Stand in warm room from 4 to 5 hours before needed. Use as soon as thawed enough to handle.
Apricots	*Purée* as apples. Alternatively, skin fruit by covering for 30 seconds in boiling water, then rub off skin. Halve and remove stone. Slice into 20 per cent lemon syrup. Leave head room in container.	1 yr	Thaw as apples. Thaw in closed container for about 3 hours at room temperature.
Avocado pears	When ripe, cut in half or slices, brush or dip in lemon juice. Freeze in usable quantities. Alternatively, wash flesh with a tablespoonful of lemon juice and freeze in small quantities.	3 mths	Thaw in wrapping at room temperature for 2½ hours and unwrap at last moment.
Bananas	Best not to attempt freezing them.		

FRUIT	METHOD	STORAGE LIFE	HOW TO THAW
Berries, blackberries cranberries blueberries gooseberries raspberries strawberries loganberries	These berries can all be frozen without sugar. Best to open freeze on trays. After about three hours, tip them into containers where they will remain loose so a few can be used at a time. It is a good idea to freeze some mixed berries for a mixed fruit pie. When freezing gooseberries, add some angelica or sweet cicely and cook them with one of these to cut down on need for sugar. Raspberries are better eaten raw. Strawberries can be quite good if caught just before they thaw, but are best used cooked. All the above berries can be frozen as a *purée* with or without sugar. I prefer not to use sugar as one tries to cut down on its use anyway and it is better to cultivate a taste for less sweet fruit.	1 yr	Thaw a little before using for pies. Strawberries are excellent with apples in a pie or crumble.
elderberries	Add flavour and food value when they are really ripe. Freeze like the flowers in a polythene bag. Pop a few in when stewing fruits for pies or jam.		
Cherries	Pit, then wash in chilled water and dry. Open freeze on trays then pack into containers.	1 yr	Stand in room temperature for several hours — can go frozen into pies.
Chestnuts	Bring nuts to boil, drain and peel then freeze. Alternatively, as a *purée*, prepare as above, but return to simmering water and cook, then sieve, cool and freeze.	1 yr 3 mths	Thaw before using.

FRUIT	METHOD	STORAGE LIFE	HOW TO THAW
Coconut, fresh	Grate coconut, freeze raw in small usable amounts.	2 mths	Thaw, or add to curries frozen.
Currants, black red white	As berries.		
Damsons	Halve and stone, open freeze, then pack. Alternatively, as a *purée*, simmer in a little water until soft, then sieve, cool and freeze.	1 yr	Use quickly from freezer as fruit discolours.
Dates, fresh	Wash, dry, stone and pack.	3 mths	Thaw at room temperature.
Elder flowers	These lovely creamy flowers are at their best for such a short time, yet they have many uses, so freezing them is ideal. Put whole, dry flowers into a polythene bag, draw out air, label and freeze.	1 yr	Put crumbled flowers into a muslin bag and use whole while still frozen. When flowers are defrosted they go black but retain their scent so can still be used.
Figs	Wash in chilled water and peel (as skin toughens when frozen). Open freeze and then pack.	3 mths	Take out carefully, thaw at room temperature.
Grapefruit	Prepare into segments separated from skin, pack in usable quantities and freeze.	1 yr	Thaw in container in fridge overnight.

FRUIT	METHOD	STORAGE LIFE	HOW TO THAW
Grapes	Seedless — wash, dry and freeze.	6 mths	Thaw for an hour at room temperature.
	Others — skin and pip, freeze in usable quantities. A whole bunch can be frozen. Wash and dry very gently, then freeze, packed in tissue paper.	2 wks	Bring out an hour before needed, setting on table still frozen.
Greengages	As damsons.		
Guava	Wash, peel and cut in half. Cook until tender in water or pineapple juice, sieve and freeze.	1 yr	Thaw at room temperature for 2 hours.
Lemons	Freeze whole to use for marmalade (note weight), or squeeze juice and freeze in ice cube trays. Alternatively, lemon peel can be grated, open frozen then removed to a polythene bag (small quantities can be used at a time) or lemon slices can be frozen in a bag — open freezing first.	1 yr	Use all frozen, straight into dishes.
Mangoes	They are best frozen in a light syrup. Wash, peel and slice straight into the syrup with a little lemon juice.	1 yr	Thaw at room temperature for about 2 hours.
Medlars	When really ripe, scoop out flesh from each fruit, mix with a very little soft brown sugar and freeze in small quantities.	1 yr	Thaw at room temperature for about 2 hours.
Melons	Wash, peel and cut melon into cubes or balls. Freeze in small quantities. They can be dipped in lemon water first.	1 yr	Thaw in fridge for about 3 hours, eat when still frosty.

FRUIT	METHOD	STORAGE LIFE	HOW TO THAW
Nectarines	Peel carefully, cut in halves or slice (under cold water helps stop discoloration) brush with lemon juice or dip in lemon water, then freeze quickly in small quantities. Can be frozen in a light syrup with a little lemon juice.	1 yr	Thaw as melons
Nuts	All nuts freeze well. They can be frozen whole, grated, chopped, ground or even toasted.	1 yr	Thaw whole nuts at room temperature for about 3 hours. Use ground and grated nuts straight from frozen.
Oranges	As lemons or grapefruit. Seville oranges for marmalade have such a short season that it is a great help to be able to freeze some instead of having to make all the marmalade in January or February. Freeze whole or prepare up to stage before sugar is added. Freeze in usable quantities, always labelling with weight.	1 yr	Add sugar and then thaw gently over low heat, stirring or allow to thaw at room temperature or in fridge.
Peaches	As nectarines.		
Pears	Not very good for freezing as they lose flavour. However, if you have a surplus of good tasty pears, try this method — Freeze when just ripe. They need to be poached in sugar syrup to maintain any flavour. Peel and quarter quickly and drop straight in to cold syrup made as follows: 1pt. boiling water to which is added 10 oz. (275g) sugar and 1 tablespoonful of lemon juice. Dissolve sugar and cool. Be sure to leave head room when putting into container.	6 mths	Thaw at room temperature for about 3 to 4 hours. Serve really cold.

FRUIT	METHOD	STORAGE LIFE	HOW TO THAW
Persimmons	Freeze whole, unpeeled fruit in foil.	2 mths	Thaw unwrapped and serve 'frosty' or fruit will darken.
Pineapples	Choose really ripe fruit. Cut in slices or chunks. If film or foil is put in between slices they can be easily separated for use a few at a time. Wrap and freeze.	1 yr	Thaw at room temperature for about 3 hours.
Plums	As greengages.		
Pomegranates	Best to freeze as juice when fruit is really ripe. Can be frozen in small containers e.g. ice cube trays, then removed and stored when frozen.	1 yr	Add to fresh fruit salads as frozen chunks.
Rhubarb	Young rhubarb can be frozen raw, just clean sticks, pack and freeze. Alternatively, cook with a few leaves of angelica or sweet cicely. Rub through a sieve, add a little brown sugar and cool and freeze.	1 yr	Add to stews and pies Thaw *purée* at room temperature until ready to use.

VEGETABLE	METHOD	STORAGE LIFE	HOW TO THAW
Artichokes (globe)	They need to be fresh and not too large. Trim outer leaves, wash thoroughly, trim stalks and take out hairy choke. Use large container, boiling water with a tablespoonful of lemon juice. Immerse for 7 minutes, drain well upside down and cool quickly.	1 yr	Plunge whole frozen artichoke into boiling water for 5 minutes or until leaves are tender.
Artichokes (Jerusalem)	They must be fresh. Peel thinly, slice and simmer in olive oil or butter, then add a little water with lemon juice, simmering until cooked. Beat to a *purée* and freeze when cold. Alternatively, cook whole in water with lemon juice, then peel and *purée*, or slice thinly, keep in water with lemon juice until enough ready to blanch and then blanch for 2 minutes.	3 mths	Add *purées* straight to soups. Plunge slices into boiling water until hot, then drain and toss in oil.
Asparagus pea	Check that they are clean. Use when small, blanch whole for 1 minute.	1 yr	Plunge into boiling water until hot.
Asparagus	Prepare as soon as possible after cutting, trim stalks and wash in cold water. Sort into size and blanch separately. Very small ones should be cooked for 3 minutes and larger ones for 4 minutes. Cool and drain thoroughly.	9 mths	Plunge into boiling water for 5 minutes, serve with butter.
Aubergines	Must be fresh and glossy, medium sized and mature. Cut into slices and blanch for 4 minutes with a little lemon juice.	6 mths	Thaw at room temperature, or fry frozen.
Beans, Broad	Use small to medium sized in perfect condition. Blanch for 1½ to 2 minutes. Treat leaf tips like spinach.	1 yr	Plunge frozen into boiling water for 6 to 8 minutes.

VEGETABLE	METHOD	STORAGE LIFE	HOW TO THAW
Beans, French Runner	Use only young beans that do not need stringing. Trim, cut or leave whole. Blanch for 2 minutes.	1 yr	Plunge from frozen into boiling water for 3 to 5 minutes.
Beetroot	Choose only small ones. They must be completely cooked or they become rubbery. Grade for size and add smaller ones as larger are cooking. Rub off skins when cooked and chilled. Freeze when cold. Make beetroot juice like apple juice — there is no need to cook but use quickly when thawed.	6 mths	Thaw in fridge.
Broccoli, white and purple	Only use good fresh plump heads, wash well, cut off stalks. Separate into small and large pieces. Blanch for 3 or 4 minutes, make sure all are in water, shake basket once or twice during blanching. Open freeze to avoid sticking together.	1 yr	Plunge frozen into boiling water for 5 to 8 minutes.
Brussels sprouts	Only freeze small compact sprouts. Trim and wash well. Blanch for 4 minutes. Pack in extra wrapping as they have a strong smell.	1 yr	Plunge frozen into boiling water for 6 to 8 minutes.
Cabbage, green or red	Winter prices often rocket so it may well be worth freezing your own cabbages. Clean and shred, blanch in water with a little lemon juice for 1½ minutes.	6 mths	Plunge into boiling water and cook for 4 minutes. Drain off water and add a little margarine. Toss for a few minutes with seasoning.
Calabrese	As for broccoli.		

VEGETABLE	METHOD	STORAGE LIFE	HOW TO THAW
Carrots	Choose only young tender carrots. Wash and clean. Leave whole if small or cut into ½-inch sections. Blanch for 3 to 4 minutes.	1 yr	Cook in a little boiling water from frozen for 5 to 8 minutes.
	Older carrots can be *puréed*. Clean, cut into small pieces, *sauté* in a little oil until soft, then mash. Alternatively, boil in water until cooked and then mash.	if with oil 6 mths	Use *purée* straight into soups and sauces.
Cauliflower	Wash and break into pieces, separate small and large florettes for blanching. Blanch for 3 to 4 minutes.	6 mths	Plunge into boiling water for 5 to 10 minutes.
Celeriac	Peel and either grate, dice or slice. Blanch with lemon juice in water for 1 minute. Can be pured like carrots.	6 mths	Do not use raw. Add frozen to soups, stews, sauces. Or cook from frozen in boiling water until soft. *Purée* can be reheated gently with a little butter or in oven.
Celery	Use crisp tender heads. Clean thoroughly, cut into 1-inch lengths. Blanch for 3 minutes and cool then freeze with blanching water.	1 yr	Thaw as celeriac.
Chicory	Choose young tight heads with yellow tips. Trim. (Use outer leaves immediately.) Blanch for 2 minutes in water with lemon juice. Drain extra carefully.	6 mths	Put into boiling water for about 15 minutes or braise from frozen.

VEGETABLE	METHOD	STORAGE LIFE	HOW TO THAW
Corn on the Cob	Must be young, fresh and tender. Husk and leave intact on the core. Trim stems down and blanch for 5 to 8 minutes, depending on size. Cut kernels from cob when cool if preferred, otherwise cool and dry well before freezing.	1 yr	Thaw before cooking, preferably in fridge, then cook in boiling water for 10 minutes. Alternatively, put into cold water, bring to fast boil on high heat, then simmer for 5 minutes.
Courgettes	Use small, new courgettes, wash and dry then cut into ½ to 1-inch lengths. Blanch for 3 minutes.	6 mths	Fry while still frozen.
Cucumber	Must be fresh. Wash, dry and slice. Can be frozen raw, or covered with equal quantities of water and cider vinegar, season with a little brown sugar and fresh black pepper.	2 mths	Thaw and use.
Fennel	Clean well, slice, blanch for 3 minutes and freeze in blanching water.	6 mths	Simmer in blanching water until tender.
Good King Henry	Treat as spinach.		
Herbs	All herbs freeze well. Gather them before the flower heads have formed and choose a still, dry day before the sun has become too hot. Take mature leaves which are more aromatic and be careful not to bruise them. It is a very good idea to freeze small bundles of mixed herbs for use in individual dishes.	6 mths	When frozen they will crumble and you can take out quantities as required to put straight into your cooking.

VEGETABLE	METHOD	STORAGE LIFE	HOW TO THAW
Kale	Use only fresh young leaves. Wash well and strip leaves from stem. Blanch for a minute. They can be chopped after blanching. Drain well.	6 mths	Put straight into boiling water for about 8 minutes.
Kohlrabi	Use only small, young, tender roots. Trim, wash and peel. If very small just clean and then blanch whole — otherwise slice. Blanch for 2 to 3 minutes.	1 yr	Plunge frozen into boiling water for 10 minutes.
Leeks	Choose medium sized, mature but not old leeks. Remove outer leaves, wash well and cut into ½-inch rings. Blanch for 2 to 3 minutes. Pack with extra wrapping.	6 mths	Add frozen to soups, sauces and stews.
Lettuce	Trim, take off any outer leaves, wash and shake dry. Blanch for 2 minutes, then cool and squeeze out any excess moisture.	6 mths	Use cooked in soups or cook with peas.
Marrow	Small marrows should be treated as courgettes. Larger ones can be peeled, seeded and cooked to a *purée*.	6 mths	Heat *purée* gently in butter, or heat in oven.
Mushrooms	Use only very fresh mushrooms in perfect condition. Small ones can be frozen as they are, just cleaned and dried. Stalks can be separated if wished. Alternatively, blanch in water with a little lemon juice for 1 minute or cook in butter or oil for 5 minutes.	3 mths	Add frozen to soups, stews or sauces, or fry gently from frozen.
Onions	Tiny onions can be blanched whole or chopped or sliced. They can be left unblanched. Wrap in extra layers as smell can penetrate.	2 mths	Add frozen to stews, soups and sauces or fry from frozen.

VEGETABLE	METHOD	STORAGE LIFE	HOW TO THAW
Parsnips	Small tender parsnips can be scrubbed and diced. Blanch for 2 minutes. Older parsnips are best *puréed*.	1 yr	Put frozen into boiling water and cook for about 10 minutes. *Purées* can be gently heated in butter or oven.
Peas	Choose young and tender peas, sort into sizes. Blanch for 1 to 1½ minutes. Freeze with some sprigs of mint which do not need blanching.	1 yr	Throw into boiling water for 3 to 5 minutes.
Peppers	Wash and dry and take out seeds. Cut in slices, rings, quarters or halves. Blanch from 2 to 3 minutes or leave whole.	1 yr	Use from frozen in sauces, stews or soups. Allow whole peppers to thaw for stuffing.
Potatoes	They are difficult, so experiment before freezing a lot. New small potatoes should be cleaned, scrubbed and boiled to nearly cooked, then cooled and frozen with a sprig of mint. Chips can be prepared by cutting up, drying then cooking in hot fat for about 4 minutes (not browned), cooled and frozen. Baked potatoes need to be cooked and have insides scooped out and stored as *purée* then reheated for about 35 minutes – so there seems to be little point in doing this. Duchesse potatoes are more worthwhile. Beat mashed potatoes with a little margarine and an egg if liked, then pipe into shapes. Open freeze and then pack.	3 mths	New potatoes should be removed from freezer about 2 hours before needed. Then gently heat in hot butter. Slightly thaw chips and dry before cooking in hot fat. Put frozen potato shapes after brushing with egg wash or milk, into medium oven for about 20 minutes.

VEGETABLE	METHOD	STORAGE LIFE	HOW TO THAW
Pumpkin	Peel and cube, cook until soft, then drain and *purée*.	6 mths	Reheat *purée* in oven or thaw for 2 hours for pies.
Salsify	Choose young, tender undamaged roots. Scrape and cut into 2 to 3-inch chunks. Keep in lemon water until there are enough to blanch. Then blanch for 4 minutes. Do not immerse in cold water, but cool in the air.	1 yr	Cook in boiling water until soft.
Shallots	As onions.		
Spinach	Wash well and discard any thick stems. Blanch for 2 minutes. Dry well and pack in usable quantities.	1 yr	Melt butter in pan, shake frozen spinach over heat to cook.
Squash	As marrow.		
Swedes	As parsnips.		
Swiss Chard	Wash well then strip leaves from stem. Treat leaves as spinach. Blanch stems separately in uniform lengths for 2 to 4 minutes.	1 yr	Cook as spinach.
Tomatoes	Can only be frozen to use cooked. Wash, dry and freeze as they are. Alternatively, *purée* by skinning and slicing and simmering until soft. Put through sieve if wished, and freeze in usable quantities.	1 yr	Put whole tomatoes in hot water for 1 minute remove skin, then slice and use. Or put straight into soups, stews or sauces. Alternatively, add frozen *purée* to soups and stews etc.
Turnips	As parsnips.		

4
PASTRY

Pastry forms the basis of many savouries and sweets. Recipes for the various types of pastry are pretty well standard, but since some readers may be unfamiliar with the use of whole flours I am including basic recipes below.

In every case 100 per cent flour can be used, but for the beginner it is a good idea to sieve out the bran and use this for something else. If you are very uncertain then there is no harm in starting off with 81 per cent flour which has more of the coarser elements taken out. But since it is far more healthful to eat the wholewheat flour I do hope that beginners in the art of wholefood cookery will gradually add more and more 100 per cent flour. Not only will it be better for health, but it really does taste a whole lot better. It is even more tasty if you grind your own wheat, and there are several very good grinders on the market.

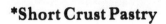

*Short Crust Pastry

225g (8 oz) 100 per cent wholewheat flour
100g (4 oz) margarine or
50g (2 oz) soft margarine and
50g (2 oz) soft white vegetable fat
4 scant tablespoonsful cold water
pinch of salt

Sieve flour and salt, adding bran in after sieving. Rub the fat into the flour until it resembles bread crumbs. Then add the water working it in as lightly as possible. Put to rest for half an hour in a cold place. Roll out on a lightly floured board.

Make sure that the pastry is soft enough since wholewheat flours usually take up more water than refined flours.

Pastry for Flan Cases
(sweet or savoury)

225g (8 oz) flour
125g (5 oz) soft margarine
1 tablespoonful soya flour
1 large egg yolk lightly beaten with
1 tablespoonful water

Proceed as for shortcrust, adding about 25g (1 oz) of soft brown sugar for a sweet flan.

*Rough Puff Pastry

**225g (8 oz) flour (100 per cent can be quite
satisfactory, a mixture gives lighter results.)
190g (6¼ oz) hard margarine or
half margarine and half hard white nut fat
1 tablespoonful soya flour
pinch of salt
10 tablespoonsful water**

Make sure that the fat is really hard by putting in fridge
several hours before needed, or in freezer for half an hour.
Grate fat on a coarse grater, and fork it into the sifted
flours and salt. Add the water holding back the last
tablespoonful if the dough is pliable enough.

It is most important to gently roll dough into an oblong
and then fold in three and put into a plastic bag and chill
for at least two hours in the fridge before using.

It can be frozen at this stage and kept for up to two
months in the freezer, then thawed at room temperature
before use. When shaping remember not to put a glaze on
the sides or the pastry will be sealed and will not rise.

CLIVE BIRCH.

Cheese Pastry

Add 50g (2 oz) grated hard cheese to shortcrust or flan pastries. The cheese should be grated on the fine grater. Parmesan can be used. The addition of half a teaspoonful of dry mustard sifted into the flour adds to the taste. One can also add a pinch of cayenne.

Cheese pastry freezes as well as ordinary pastry.

*Herb Pastry

A large handful of mixed herbs put through a mouli sieve gives an interesting taste to pastry.

*Savoury Pastry

Rub in a teaspoonful of yeast extract when incorporating the fat into the flour.

A Biscuit Type of Crust

To the short pastry recipe add 50g (2 oz) soft brown sugar and a small egg instead of the water.

Chou Pastry

Although this can be made using 100 per cent flour with the bran sieved out, it is much better if a lighter flour is used. Exchanging 25g (1 oz) of flour with a strong white unbleached flour produces a really tasty pastry. Chou made with completely refined flour has virtually no taste and relies on the filling!

70g (2½ oz) flour
60g (just over 2¼ oz) margarine
150ml (¼ pt) milk or water
pinch of salt
2 eggs
¼ teaspoonful sugar, and a little vanilla essence if for sweet pastry

Sieve the flour, and then warm it. Have it ready to handle quickly.

Boil the liquid with the fat and add salt and sugar. When it is boiling fast take it off the heat and immediately shoot in the flour beating it into the liquid mixture as you do so. Beat to a smooth panade. It is ready when the paste leaves the sides of the pan quite smooth. It should be glossy and firm and able to stand up in peaks.

Put the mixture into a piping bag and use as required.

When formed, choux pastry should be cooked in an oven at 200°C/400°F (Gas Mark 6) for about 20 minutes and then the heat can be reduced a little until the pastry is quite crisp at the sides. When the shapes come out of the oven they should be slit open and any soft paste inside scooped out with the handle of a spoon.

Chou pastry needs to be eaten on the day it is cooked or it becomes soft and soggy. However it freezes well, and can be filled and frozen or carefully frozen as it is and filled as it thaws. This it does very quickly.

Chou pastry cannot be frozen uncooked.

5
CHEESE

Cheese and Potato Bake

**450g (1 lb) potatoes
1 medium onion, sliced and separated into rings
25g (1 oz) margarine
150g (5 oz) cheddar cheese, grated
2 sticks celery, chopped into small pieces
salt and pepper**

Cook the cleaned potatoes in boiling water for 15 minutes.
Drain and cool enough to peel off skins, and slice thickly.
Sauté onion rings and celery in margarine for five minutes.
Layer potatoes, onion and celery and cheese in an
ovenproof dish, finishing with cheese and seasoning as
wished. Cook to heat through and brown top in oven
220°C/400°F (Gas Mark 6) for about 15 minutes. This
makes a good supper dish or can be served with salad.

To freeze: Line dish with foil or use oven/freezer dish.

Storage life: 2 months.

To thaw: Put straight into oven as above, but cook for
   three quarters of an hour and be sure dish is heated
   through. Top can be covered with foil to begin with and
   this taken away for last 15 minutes.

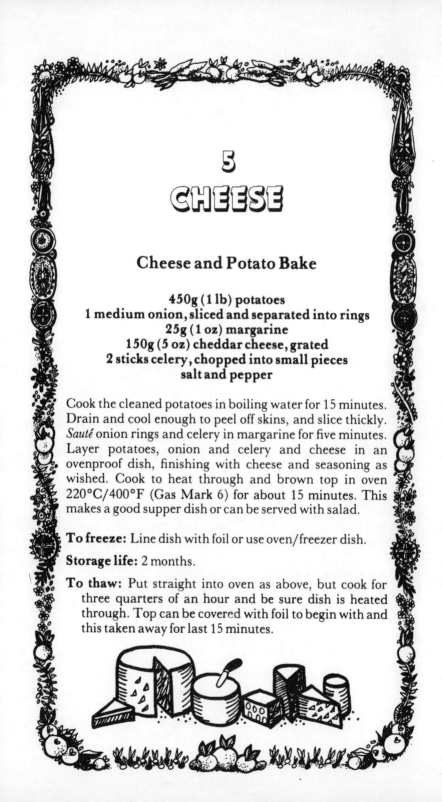

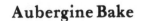

Aubergine Bake

**4 medium-sized aubergines
25g (1 oz) margarine
salt and pepper**

Topping:
**200 ml (8 fl oz) milk
3 large eggs, lightly beaten
100g (4 oz) Edam cheese, grated and mixed with a
teaspoonful dry mustard
1 small onion, chopped
good sprig of parsley, chopped**

Cut the aubergines in two lengthways, score across and sprinkle with salt. Turn them upside down onto a plate for 30 minutes. Then drain and wipe dry. Place the aubergines tightly together in a fairly deep ovenproof dish. Place knobs of margarine over and bake for ten minutes in oven at 190°C/375°F (Gas Mark 5).

Bring milk to just under boiling point then whisk in the eggs, cheese and seasoning. Sprinkle chopped onion over the aubergines then pour egg mixture over. Return to oven, reducing heat to 180°C/350°F (Gas Mark 4) for about 50 minutes or until the top is baked. Serve with potatoes and green vegetables.

To freeze: Prepare and cook aubergines, but before cooking line dish with foil. When aubergines are cool, open freeze in dish. Then remove dish, wrap and label. Put this into a polythene bag with grated cheese already seasoned and with mustard. The eggs can be beaten with a little salt and frozen.

Storage: 2 to 3 months.

To thaw: Remove foil from aubergines and return to original dish. Prepare custard, chop onion and proceed as above. (If eggs have been frozen they will need to be thawed in advance.) Allow extra time in oven if aubergines go in frozen.

Celeriac Potato Boats

½ kilo (1 lb) potatoes
1 small celeriac, coarsely grated
25g (1 oz) margarine
150g (5 oz) Edam cheese, grated
1 lemon
salt and pepper

Clean potatoes and boil in a little salted water until soft, then remove from water and take off skin when cool enough to handle (or if young keep skin on). Cut lemon in half and put one half aside. Use juice of half to add to water and simmer celeriac until it is soft, adding more water if necessary.

Mash potatoes with margarine and seasoning. Form into boat shapes on a greased tray. Piping gives the best appearance. Potatoes can be mashed with addition of a small egg if wished. Mix drained celeriac with most of the cheese and heap this into the boats. Sprinkle the rest of the cheese on top.

Put into medium oven 180°C/350°F (Gas Mark 4) for 10-15 minutes or put under the grill until cheese is melted and golden. Serve with slices of lemon twisted on each boat.

To freeze: Prepare but do not put in oven, open freeze and then wrap. Freeze half lemon whole or sliced, wrapped in film.

Storage life: 3 to 4 months.

To thaw: Thaw at room temperature for two hours then put in oven to heat.

Cheese Flan

One deep pastry case – short crust pastry (see page 40)
175g (6 oz) hard cheese, grated
50g (2 oz) flour, 100 per cent
50g (2 oz) margarine
275ml ($\frac{1}{2}$ pt) milk
1 egg
$\frac{1}{2}$ teaspoonful mustard
pinch cayenne
salt and pepper

Blend the flour with the fat. Bring the milk to nearly boiling and then, very gradually at first, pour the milk onto the mixture, beating it in. When it is well mixed beat in the egg. Then stir in most of the cheese, and seasonings.

Return to the rinsed saucepan and stir over a low heat until it thickens. Then pour into the pastry case and sprinkle the rest of the cheese on top. This looks attractive if it is done in regular lines. Cook in oven 200°C/400°F (Gas Mark 6) for about 30 minutes or until pastry is cooked and top golden.

To freeze: Allow to cool then open freeze and pack. The flan freezes well before being cooked.

Storage life: 3 months.

To thaw: Thaw at room temperature for about 3 hours or put straight into the oven giving extra time if flan was not cooked. Cover top for part of the time.
This flan is good eaten hot or cold.

Cheese Pudding

175g (6 oz) hard cheese, grated (can include
tablespoonful parmesan cheese)
25g (1 oz) 81 per cent flour
25g (1 oz) margarine
275 ml ($\frac{1}{2}$ pt) milk
2 medium eggs
1 teaspoonful dry mustard
salt and pepper

Make a thick sauce with fat, flour and milk, stir for a few
minutes to cook, then take off heat and cool a little. Beat in
the eggs then stir in cheese and seasonings. Put into a well
greased dish and bake in oven set at 180°C/350°F (Gas
Mark 4) for about 45 minutes until well set.

This dish will not freeze well when it is cooked, but can
be frozen raw.

To freeze: Pour into foil or freezer/oven dish, wrap and
freeze.

Storage life: 1 month.

To serve: Put straight into the oven from the freezer, bake
for an extra 15 to 20 minutes.

Variations on Cheese Pudding

Tomato cheese pudding. Put several sliced tomatoes at
bottom of well greased dish, sprinkle over with a little
basil. Add a teaspoonful of tomato *purée* to the cheese
mixture.

Mushroom cheese pudding. Grease the dish extra well, and
line the bottom with cleaned, dry mushrooms, sprinkle
with a little fresh, black pepper and a grate of nutmeg.

Freeze variations in the same way.

Cheese and Tomato Flan

Ingredients as for cheese flan but reduce the amount of cheese to 75g (3 oz) and add two large skinned and sliced tomatoes. Make the filling as described, place the tomatoes in a circle on the bottom of the flan before adding the filling. The tomatoes tend to rise to the top so it is a good idea to reserve some cheese and put this on top about five minutes before the flan is cooked.

Freezing is the same, but if the tomatoes are at the top they tend to shrink in freezing, and this does not look so attractive. In this case, when reheating the flan, sprinkle more cheese on top, or add another layer of tomatoes covering them with cheese.

Cheese and Onion Flan

Ingredients as for cheese flan with the addition of one medium sized onion cut into rings. Make the filling as described, place the onions in a pattern on the bottom of the flan case before adding the filling.

This flan looks nice with extra onion rings on top. Take about eight even-sized rings, dip them in milk and then a little seasoned flour. Fry these in shallow fat on both sides, and then arrange on top of the flan when it is cooked. Sprinkle a small amount of cheese over and return to the oven for about five minutes.

Onion flan freezes in the same way as cheese flan.

Cheesey Hazel Nut Roll

**100g (4 oz) hazelnuts, chopped and roasted
50g (2 oz) oatflakes, toasted carefully under grill
75g (3 oz) pineapple chunks, chopped
2 small tomatoes, skinned and chopped
shortcrust pastry made with the addition of grated
cheese**

Make the pastry (see page 40) and allow it to rest in the fridge or cold place for half an hour.

Prepare ingredients and mix them lightly together. Roll out the pastry to an oblong about 6 ins x 12 ins. Put the mixture in the centre and damp edges, rolling pastry to enclose mixture. With joined edges underneath transfer to a baking sheet. Glaze the top with egg or milk, and cut diagonal slashes along the top.

Bake in oven 200°C/400°F (Gas Mark 6) for 30 minutes. Good hot or cold.

To freeze: Cool, open freeze and then wrap, or prepare to rolling stage, then open freeze and wrap.

Storage life: 2 months.

To thaw: Thaw overnight in fridge or for shorter time at room temperature. Or put straight into the oven as above giving extra time if pastry was raw. Cover top if necessary to avoid burning.

Mushroom Cheese Drops

100g (4 oz) hard cheese, grated
25g (1 oz scant) flour 100 per cent
1 dessertspoonful soya flour
25g (1 oz) margarine
150ml ¼ pt water
1 large egg
50g (2 oz) mushrooms
oil, salt and pepper

Chop and *sauté* the mushrooms in a little oil, dry them on kitchen paper. Make a very thick white sauce with fat, flours and milk, stir for a few minutes to cook, then take off heat and cool a little. Beat in the egg, then stir in cheese and seasoning. Add the mushrooms. Heat a little oil in the frying pan and drop good teaspoonful of mixture onto the fat. Turn after a few minutes. Serve hot with potatoes and mixed vegetables.

Method 1

To freeze: Raw mixture can be frozen, but must be put into a container and frozen quickly or it tends to discolour. Freeze in a flat shape for quick freezing and thawing.

Storage life: 1 month.

To thaw: Leave at room temperature in container for two hours then cook as above.

Method 2

To freeze: Freeze cooked drops on plate when cold and cover well.

Storage life: 1 month.

To thaw: Put frozen drops in a little hot fat and heat through.

Mushroom and Cream Cheese Pie

225g (8 oz) pastry, flaky is best but shortcrust will do
(see page 40)
225g (8 oz) cream cheese
50g (2 oz) sliced roasted almonds
100g (4 oz) mushrooms, sliced
3 tomatoes, skinned and chopped
1 small red pepper, diced
1 small raw beetroot, grated fine (use gloves)
1 little fresh oregano or basil, chopped
salt and pepper
grate of nutmeg
beaten egg for glaze

Line a shallow pie dish with the pastry, setting enough aside for a lid. Beat the cheese with the beetroot and tomatoes until smooth, then mix in all the other ingredients. Season and let down with a little water if the mixture is too stiff.

Put into pie shell. Make a top and seal it with water. Use trimmings for decoration. Brush with beaten egg (do not brush sides if using flaky pastry as it will then not rise). Bake for 40 minutes in oven 200°C/400°F (Gas Mark 6).

To freeze: Cool and freeze in the dish, or freeze raw.

Storage life: 2 months.

To thaw: Thaw overnight and then reheat in a moderate oven taking care to cover top to avoid burning. Or put straight into oven from frozen and reheat. If raw allow an extra half an hour's cooking time.

N.B. This is very quick to prepare and for the odd occasion bought, frozen flaky pastry could be used. Ingredients are marked on the package and a vegetarian brand can be obtained (Jus-Rol).

Quick Cheese Soufflé

50g (2 oz) plain 81 per cent flour
50g (2 oz) margarine or butter
175g (6 oz) cheddar cheese, grated
2 tablespoonsful parmesan cheese
3 medium eggs
550ml (1 pt) milk, heated to nearly boiling
½ teaspoonful dry mustard
salt and pepper

Put all the ingredients, except mustard and cheese, in liquidizer, blend at highest speed until well mixed. Mix mustard into cheeses, and then add these gradually to the mixture.

Pour into well greased dish (this is enough for two pint sized dishes or one large one). Cook in oven at 200°C/400°F (Gas Mark 6) for 45 minutes. This will not rise as much as a normal *soufflé*, but looks good just the same.

To freeze: Do not freeze cooked dish, but it is possible to freeze uncooked mixture. Line the dish in which it will eventually be cooked with foil, freeze, then remove dish and wrap.

Storage life: 3 months.

To thaw: Return to well greased dish, if in a great hurry put straight into oven and give extra time to cook, otherwise thaw first.

6
EGGS

Scotch Eggs

4 hard boiled eggs
split bea burger mixture (page 77) or lentil mixture
(page 78) or nut savoury mixture (page 87)
Egg and crumbs (oatflakes, sesame seeds are good)
oil

Cook the eggs and dip immediately in cold water to facilitate shelling. Cover them with a thin layer of chosen mixture. Egg and crumb. Fry in deep fat. If frying in shallow fat, move round and baste. (But this is not so satisfactory). Cut in halves and serve hot or cold.

To freeze: Hard boiled eggs cannot be frozen, but the chosen mixture can be frozen in a thin flat oblong shape.

Storage life: 3 months.

To thaw: Leave at room temperature for about an hour, then proceed as above.

Vegetarian Sausage and Egg Plate Pie

**4 vegetarian sausages either tinned or home-made
2 medium-sized eggs
1 small bunch parsley, chopped
pastry made with 100 per cent flour
salt and pepper**

Divide pastry into two for lining a large pie plate and covering top. Cut the sausages in half and arrange on the pastry on the plate. Beat eggs with parsley and seasoning and pour over the sausages. Damp pastry edges and cover with rest of pastry, decorating the top and sealing the edges. Brush with a little egg. Bake in oven 200°C/400°F (Gas Mark 6) for 30 minutes or until the pastry is browned a little.

To freeze: Allow to cool, open freeze and then remove plate, supporting pie with a cardboard plate if liked. Alternatively, freeze uncooked.

Storage life: 2 months.

To thaw: Return to plate and thaw in fridge overnight or at room temperature for several hours. Alternatively, put straight into a moderate oven to heat through. If frozen raw allow an extra 20 to 30 minutes to cook right through.

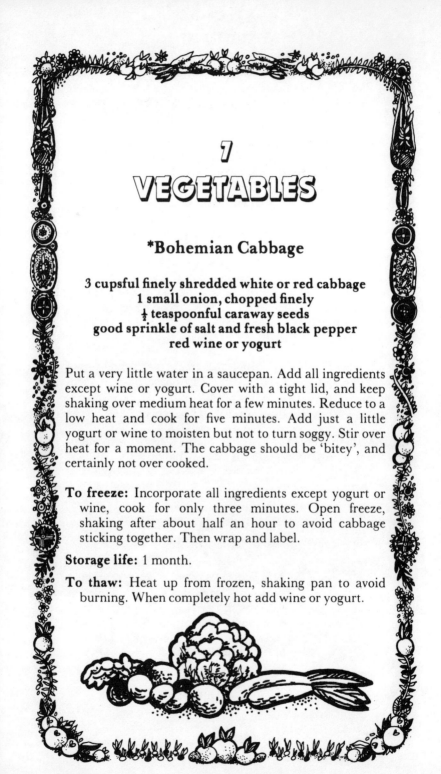

1
VEGETABLES

*Bohemian Cabbage

**3 cupsful finely shredded white or red cabbage
1 small onion, chopped finely
½ teaspoonful caraway seeds
good sprinkle of salt and fresh black pepper
red wine or yogurt**

Put a very little water in a saucepan. Add all ingredients except wine or yogurt. Cover with a tight lid, and keep shaking over medium heat for a few minutes. Reduce to a low heat and cook for five minutes. Add just a little yogurt or wine to moisten but not to turn soggy. Stir over heat for a moment. The cabbage should be 'bitey', and certainly not over cooked.

To freeze: Incorporate all ingredients except yogurt or wine, cook for only three minutes. Open freeze, shaking after about half an hour to avoid cabbage sticking together. Then wrap and label.

Storage life: 1 month.

To thaw: Heat up from frozen, shaking pan to avoid burning. When completely hot add wine or yogurt.

*Apple Savoury

175g (6 oz) mushrooms, preferably large ones
2 large carrots, sliced thinly
1 large parsnip, diced into small cubes
oil
150ml (¼ pt) apple juice
salt and pepper
grate of nutmeg
2 tablespoonsful chopped mint and thyme
1 clove of garlic, crushed
75g (3 oz) almonds cut into slivers

Just cover the bottom of a saucepan with oil, add the mushroom tops whole and stalks chopped. Fry for about five minutes until mushrooms are cooked, then take tops out and put on a plate and keep warm. Add garlic, carrots and parsnip, simmer for a few minutes, then carefully pour in the apple juice. Cover and cook for about five minutes until it is all cooked, and season to taste. If there is any excess liquid pour this off and use for a delicious tomato sauce.

Transfer ingredients to a heated fireproof dish, arrange mushrooms on top then sprinkle nuts on, put under grill for two or three minutes to brown nuts.

To freeze: Cool and freeze whole dish, or keep mushrooms and rest separate.

Storage time: 2 months.

To thaw: Dish can be put into an oven and heated through. Alternatively, gently heat carrot mixture through in saucepan then transfer to dish, put mushrooms on top and put under grill, after about five minutes turn mushrooms over and return to grill and, after another five minutes, sprinkle nuts on top and finish under grill.

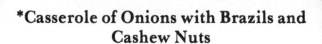

*Casserole of Onions with Brazils and Cashew Nuts

4 large onions, sliced
1 cupful mixed brazils and cashew nuts, chopped
3 tablespoonsful oil
1 tablespoonful fresh chopped mint
salt and pepper

Grease a casserole layer in all the ingredients except the oil which should be poured over the top to cover. Put on lid and bake in oven 180°C/350°F (Gas Mark 4) for an hour, or until onion is cooked.

To freeze: Cool completely, open freeze then remove from casserole and pack well.

Storage life: 1 month.

To thaw: Remove wrapping and return to original dish. Leave overnight in fridge. Heat thoroughly in oven. Can be transferred to saucepan or double boiler and heated more quickly but this is less satisfactory.

Onion Flan with Artichokes and Tomato

1 flan case baked blind (see pastry section)
3 medium onions, skinned and sliced thinly
100g (4 oz) artichokes
1 tomato, skinned and sliced finely
2 large eggs
150ml ($\frac{1}{4}$ pt) milk
25g (1 oz) 100 per cent flour
25g (1 oz) margarine
salt and pepper

Clean and cook artichokes in water with a little lemon juice, then cool and skin. *Sauté* onion in margarine for about five minutes. Beat eggs into milk, with flour (use liquidizer for this or blend a little milk into flour first and gradually add more and then add eggs). Season milk mixture.

Cover bottom of flan case with onions, slice artichoke on top and lastly arrange rings of tomato round centre. Pour over milk mixture. Bake in oven 180°C/350°F (Gas Mark 4) 20 to 30 minutes.

To freeze: Open freeze and then wrap and label.

Storage life: 2 months.

To thaw: Put in oven frozen, covering top, for about 50 minutes or until heated through.

*Picnic Pies

**Pastry made with 225g (8 oz) 100 per cent flour (see
page 40)
50g (2 oz) cashew nuts
50g (2 oz) millet flakes
50g (2 oz) sprouted chick peas, chopped
1 onion, chopped
1 large tomato, skinned and chopped
100g (4 oz) sweet corn kernels, cooked
2 tablespoonsful tomato** *purée*
**1 tablespoonful fresh basil, chopped
salt and pepper**

Make the pastry and rest it in the fridge for half an hour
while you are preparing the filling. Mix all filling
ingredients together, moisten with a little water if it
seems too dry.

Roll out the pastry and line eight small patty tins. Fill
each, then cover with pastry tops, being sure to seal well.
Decorate the tops and cut a little hole in the centre.
Brush with milk or egg if wished.

Cook in oven 200°C/400°F (Gas Mark 6) for 30
minutes. Serve hot or cold.

To freeze: Cool, open freeze and then wrap.
Alternatively, freeze before baking.

Storage life: 2 months.

To thaw: Thaw overnight in fridge or for longer at room
temperature. Be sure pies are well thawed if eating
cold. Otherwise put in moderate oven to heat. Or put
straight into oven as recipe, allowing extra time if pies
were frozen raw.

*Potato Surprise

4 good-sized potatoes
100g (4 oz) brazil nuts, medium ground
1 large tomato, skinned and chopped
1 stick celery, chopped very fine
2 heaped tablespoonsful stuffing mixture (can be
sage and onion or lemon and thyme)
2 tablespoonsful fresh mint, chopped
salt and pepper
water
oil

Scrub the potatoes clean, score with a fork. Chop off top third. Take a little off the bottom so potatoes will stand up. Hollow out the centre (use scrapings for soup). Mix stuffing mixture with all other ingredients, adding a little water if needed to make a soft consistency. Fill potatoes and return tops. Brush with oil. Wrap carefully in foil and stand in a baking tin. Bake in a hot oven for about three-quarters of an hour or until cooked.

To freeze: Cook for only half an hour. Cool and freeze.

Storage life: 1 month.

To thaw: Put straight into hot oven from freezer and cook for an hour. Make sure potatoes are well cooked before serving.

*Red Cabbage Rolls with Nut Stuffing

6 large leaves of red cabbage
100g (4 oz) hazel nuts, ground
25g (1 oz) soya flour
1 leek, cleaned and chopped (set aside dark part for soup)
4 heaped tablespoonsful cooked field beans (or any other kind of bean)
2 ripe tomatoes, skinned and chopped
1 small sprig fresh rosemary or ¼ teaspoonful dried
25g (1 oz) margarine, melted
juice of 1 small lemon
1 small tin tomato juice
salt and pepper

Immerse cabbage leaves in boiling water and add a tablespoonful of lemon juice. Bring back to boil for two minutes. Remove and refresh in cold water, drain and set aside.

To remove leaves easily the whole cabbage can be treated as above, and then leaves will come away without breaking.

Mix nuts and soya together then beat in the beans, melted margarine, tomato and leek. Add chopped rosemary, salt and pepper and a little lemon juice. Add a little of the liquid from beans (or water) if necessary to make a stiffish dropping consistency.

Stuff leaves by putting some mixture near stalk end (cutting 'V' in stalk to facilitate folding) then fold sides over and roll up, tucking end underneath.

Place stuffed leaves in a greased oven dish with a lid. Mix rest of lemon juice and tomato juice together and pour gently over all cabbage leaves. Cover and bake in oven 180°C/350°F (Gas Mark 4) for an hour (baste leaves with juice once or twice).

To freeze: Cool and freeze in dish or line dish with foil first, open freeze and then remove dish and wrap and label. Alternatively, freeze uncooked.

Storage life: 4 months.

To thaw: In each case this dish can be thawed at room temperature after removing wrapping and returning to original dish or it can be put straight into the oven and heated for half an hour in moderate oven, taking care top does not burn. Alternatively, if frozen uncooked, cook as original recipe allowing an extra 30 minutes.

*Sweet and Sour Carrots

450g (1 lb) carrots, diced
50g (2 oz) raisins
3 tablespoonsful lemon juice
¼ teaspoonful dry mustard
1 tablespoonful caraway seeds
25g (1 oz) 100 per cent flour
salt and pepper

Cook the carrots in a little water until just tender. Drain and keep hot. Add all the other ingredients to the carrot water and cook until the mixture thickens. Add more water if necessary to make a thick sauce. Serve hot over the carrots, with slices of lemon.

To freeze: Transfer to container and freeze.

Storage life: 3 months.

To thaw: Thaw in fridge or at room temperature or put into moderate oven from frozen.

*Sweet and Sour Parsnips

Recipe exactly as that for sweet and sour carrots. Good also with chopped dried apricots instead of raisins.

This recipe can be adapted for a variety of vegetables and is good as an unusual way of serving vegetables with savoury dishes, such as nut roast.

*Vegetable Pasties

**450g (1 lb) of shortcrust pastry, made with bran sifted
out of 100 per cent flour (see page 40)
50g (2 oz) brazil nuts, ground fine
1 large onion, chopped
1 large carrot, sliced
1 small parsnip, diced small
3 tablespoonsful cooked peas (can be frozen, added
straight from freezer)
2 tomatoes, skinned and chopped
1 tablespoonful whole semolina
1 teaspoonful tahini
1 tablespoonful fresh thyme, chopped or ¼
teaspoonful dried thyme
1 bay leaf
salt and pepper
a little oil
water**

Make the pastry and chill in the fridge for half an hour.
Put a little oil in a saucepan and add onion, carrot,
parsnip and shake for a few moments, then add bay leaf,
peas, seasoning and enough water to just cover.

Simmer with tight lid for five minutes. Remove
vegetables from the pan and set aside, retaining liquid in
pan. Sprinkle semolina over remaining liquid, add tahini
and tomatoes and cook stirring until the mixture
thickens, adding a little more water if needed to obtain a
thick but easily stirred consistency. Remove bay leaf.
Return vegetables to pan, mix in the ground nuts.

Roll out pastry fairly thinly. Cut into circles. Place
some of the mixture in centre of each circle, damp edges
and draw up across the centre, crimp edges by twisting
between finger and thumb. Brush pasties with milk or
plant milk, pierce tops of each to make a small hole.
Cook in oven 200°C/400°F (Gas Mark 6) for ten
minutes, then reduce to 180°C/350°F (Gas Mark 4) and
continue for another 20 minutes. Serve hot or cold.

Method 1

To freeze: Cool completely, wrap individually in foil or film, label and freeze.

Storage life: 3 months.

To thaw: Leave in fridge overnight in wrappings then heat in a moderate oven for 20-30 minutes. If to be eaten cold, make sure the pasties are at room temperature, for at least 2 hours after having been in fridge.

Method 2

To freeze: As in method 1 but to be done before cooking.

Storage life: 3 months.

To thaw: Put straight into oven, cooking as in recipe but allowing an extra ten minutes at the beginning and an extra ten minutes on the lower heat.

8
SOYA PROTEIN

Textured vegetable protein, often called soya protein, is not generally used much by vegetarians or wholefood eaters. The former often feel that vegetarian diets were perfectly adequate before the advent of 'textured vegetables' and in any case they do not want food that resembles meat in any way. Wholefood eaters frequently prefer to eat unprocessed food and they would rather eat straight soya beans.

However, many people do find soya protein a useful part of their diet. It is particularly good for those who want to give up the use of meat, but still like to make favourite recipes. For this reason, and because soya protein is an excellent source of natural nutrition, I include a few recipes here.

Soya protein freezes very well, but since it is long keeping in its dry state there would be no point in storing it in the freezer other than in made-up dishes. In such dishes the soya protein must be completely hydrated and ready for eating.

*Casserole of Vegetables with Soya Protein

75g (3 oz) chunky soya protein
50g (2 oz) green whole lentils
25g (1 oz) whole rice
25g (1 oz) whole barley
1 large onion, sliced
1 large carrot, sliced
3 sticks celery, cut into thin, 1½-inch sticks
small piece turnip, diced
1 large parsnip, diced
4 tablespoonsful tomato *purée*
1 tablespoonful of tahini
fresh herbs as available, such as mint, parsley,
thyme, sage or ½ teaspoonful mixed dried herbs
3 tablespoonsful oil
3 tablespoonsful concentrated fruit juice
salt and pepper
boiling water

Sauté all the vegetables in the oil for a few minutes then add lentils rice and barley, shake to cover then add all other ingredients except soya protein and fruit juice. Mix then cover with boiling water. Add soya protein and, if necessary, a little more water to completely cover all ingredients. Simmer on a low heat for 30 minutes or put into casserole in oven 180°C/350°F (Gas Mark 4) for an hour. Add fruit juce just before ready to serve.

To freeze: Remove from heat ten minutes early. Cool completely and freeze.

Storage life: 1 month.

To thaw: Put in container overnight in fridge or stand at room temperature for two hours then gently heat in pan taking care to keep moving at first so as not to burn.

Alternatively, return to casserole when thawed and cook for further 30 minutes.

*Cauliflower Casserole

1 large cauliflower, separated into florets
2 large onions, sliced
225g (8 oz) mushrooms, sliced
100g (4 oz) soya protein, mince type
3 large tomatoes, sliced
2 tablespoonsful tomato *purée*
$\frac{1}{2}$ teaspoonful cinnamon
good grate of nutmeg
4 tablespoonsful oil
2 tablespoonsful fresh thyme, minced or $\frac{1}{2}$
teaspoonful dried thyme
salt and pepper
275ml ($\frac{1}{2}$ pt) tomato sauce (see page 111)
water

Sauté the onion in oil for five minutes, then add mushrooms for another five minutes, turning to brown. Add all ingredients except soya protein, sauce and water. Toss in pan over heat for a few minutes. Then turn into casserole, add soya and sauce and then enough water to only just cover. Put on a tight lid and cook at 170°C/325°F (Gas Mark 3) for three to four hours, or at bottom of oven while other things are cooking. This dish can also be cooked in a saucepan on top of cooker, or in a slow cooker at low for 8 hours.

Method 1
To freeze: Cool, transfer to another container, freeze.

Storage life: 2 to 3 months.

To thaw: Thaw at room temperature for about eight hours or overnight in fridge.

Method 2
To freeze: Freeze in casserole and then wrap and label. (Line casserole with foil first if wished.)

Storage life: 2 to 3 months.

To thaw: Reheat from frozen in oven 190°C/375°F (Gas Mark 5) for 1-1$\frac{1}{2}$ hours.

*Chunky Almond Pie

225g (8 oz) mushrooms, sliced
150g (5 oz) chunks of soya protein
100g (4 oz) almonds, sliced and toasted
3 sticks celery, chopped
1 onion, sliced
50g (2 oz) margarine
25g (1 oz) 100 per cent flour
150ml (¼ pt) milk or plant milk
salt and pepper
1 tablespoonful fresh fennel, chopped
water
Pastry to cover casserole

Sauté the onion, celery and mushrooms in the margarine for about five minutes, then add the flour, stir well and cook for three minutes, add seasoning and fennel. Stir in the milk and cook until the mixture thickens. Add enough water to make quite thin consistency and then add the dry soya protein. Mix well. Take away from heat and leave while you prepare the pastry.

Turn into a casserole adding the toasted almonds. Top with pastry, fluting the edges and decorating to look attractive. Cook in oven at 200°C/400°F (Gas Mark 6) for 25 to 30 minutes.

To freeze: Cool and freeze in dish.

Storage life: 2 months.

To thaw: Thaw overnight in fridge, or put straight into a moderate oven for about 1½ hours, covering top.

*Cider Savoury

150g (5 oz) chunky soya protein (flavoured variety)
150ml (¼ pt) cider or apple juice
225g (8 oz) cooking apples, peeled, cored and thickly
sliced
1 tablespoonful dark brown sugar
1 cupful brazil nuts, coarsely grated and toasted
25g (1 oz) margarine
salt and pepper

Poach apples in cider with sugar for five minutes. Hydrate soya protein in liquid for half an hour and drain. When they are fully plumped up press out as much liquid as possible and drain on absorbent paper. Heat margarine in frying pan and fry chunks until browned and crisp on outside.

Grease a casserole dish, place in alternate layers, apple and chunks and nuts. Season as liked, last layer should be nuts. Pour any remaining liquid over and cook covered in oven 190°C/375°F (Gas Mark 5) for 30 minutes.

To freeze: Prepare but do not cook in oven. Cool and freeze either leaving in casserole or lining it with foil and removing dish when frozen.

Storage life: 4 months.

To thaw: Put straight into oven if in suitable container or return to original dish. Leave for a while before placing in heat. Can be thawed in refrigerator overnight and then cooked. If cooking from cold add an extra 10 to 15 minutes.

*Village Pie

450g (1 lb) cooked mashed potatoes
2 large onions, chopped
2 large carrots, grated
1 medium parsnip, grated
3 tomatoes, skinned and chopped
25g (1 oz) margarine
1 packet minced soya protein (can be bought in small
packets to be used as an extender for meat dishes)
1 tablespoonful tomato *purée*
1 teaspoonful mixed dried herbs
pinch cinnamon
pinch ginger
salt and pepper

Cook the onion and grated vegetables in the margarine until they are soft, taking care not to burn. Add all other ingredients except soya protein and potato. Simmer gently for 10 minutes then add the soya protein. Moisten with a little water if the mixture is too dry and cook for three minutes. Transfer the mixture to a greased dish, put the hot potato on top and fork the top into a pattern. Put into a hot oven 220°C/425°F (Gas Mark 7) for long enough to brown potatoes, or do this under the grill.

To freeze: Put finished dish into freezer when cool, freeze then pack and label. Or line the dish with foil before transferring the mixture, freeze and remove dish.

Storage life: 2 to 4 weeks. (The addition of a well beaten egg to the mashed potato improves keeping qualities.)

To thaw: Put straight into low oven for about an hour or until the dish is hot, raise heat or put under grill to brown top.

9

BEANS AND PULSES

All beans and pulses store in their dry state for many months, and so there is no need to store in the freezer. Nevertheless possessing a freezer may mean that you will make more use of these relatively cheap and highly nutritious food stuffs. They store well because they are hard and dry; but it is this very quality that often inhibits their use. Although actual preparation is easy one has to remember long beforehand that they must be soaked and then cooked.

With a freezer you can do the preparation at a convenient time, soaking and cooking a much larger quantity than is usable at once. The rest can be packed in thin rectangular shapes for quick freezing and fast thawing. Label them with weight when cooked to facilitate using straight away in recipes.

To thaw leave overnight in container in fridge or for 2 to 3 hours at room temperature. You can put them straight into stews, casseroles etc. from the freezer. Storage life in freezer is twelve months.

Beans and Digestion

Some people complain that they cannot eat beans as they are indigestible. This is a shame as there are so many types of beans and pulses which can give interesting variations to the diet. They are also cheap and easy to prepare and so especially good for older people on a strict budget. However, they are often the very ones who say they cannot eat beans.

The following method helps to make beans more digestible. Soak overnight, drain off all liquid, wash beans and then keep moist for 24 to 48 hours. Wash several times during that time. Finally wash again, then

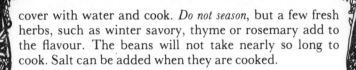

cover with water and cook. *Do not season*, but a few fresh herbs, such as winter savory, thyme or rosemary add to the flavour. The beans will not take nearly so long to cook. Salt can be added when they are cooked.

Pressure Cooker

The time element is greatly reduced by using a pressure cooker. Unless you want to use my long term soaking method you do not need to soak overnight.

Simply cover the beans with boiling water, cover on top with a plate for one hour. Drain off the water. Put 1 litre (2 pints) of water to 450g (1 lb) of beans in the pressure cooker, bring water to the boil and then add the beans. Put on lid and bring to top pressure. Cook larger beans for 30 minutes, smaller 20 minutes, lentils and split peas for 15 minutes and allow to cool to room temperature.

Beans that have been treated in my long term way will take less time than above in the pressure cooker.

Slow Cooker

Beans and pulses can also be cooked by the slow cooker method. The long soaking and washing method is best. Add boiling water to the beans and start at the high setting for an hour then six hours at low. Otherwise, cook for eight hours at low.

Butter Bean Timbale

450g (1 lb) butter beans
3 large ripe tomatoes, skinned and chopped
1 medium red pepper, seeded and sliced
2 eggs
50g (2 oz) margarine
1 leaf fresh basil, chopped
1 good sprig parsley, chopped or ¼ teaspoonful each
dried
salt and pepper

Soak beans overnight, cook and mash while still hot, beat in margarine, herbs and seasoning. Cool a little then add the beaten eggs and lastly tomatoes and pepper. Add salt and pepper as liked.

Put into a well greased basin, cover with greased paper and then foil and steam for 1 hour. Or put into shallow greased dish and bake in oven 200°C/400°F (Gas Mark 6) for 40 minutes.

To serve, turn out and serve with a tomato sauce and a variety of green vegetables.

Method 1

To freeze: Steam for 40 minutes or bake for 20 minutes, then cool and open freeze, then pack and label.

Storage life: 3 months.

To thaw: Thaw for two hours at room temperature and then steam for 40 minutes or bake for 30 minutes.

Method 2

To freeze: Do not cook at all, but cool the mixture and pack into container in which it is to be cooked.

Storage life: 3 months.

To thaw: Allow to thaw and then steam for an hour and twenty minutes or bake from frozen for an hour until cooked.

Field Bean Croquettes

225g (8 oz) field beans, soaked and cooked
1 medium onion, chopped
1 medium carrot, chopped
1 egg, beaten
150ml (¼ pt) liquid from beans (or water)
1 tablespoonful vegetarian worcester sauce
(Holbrook's)
2 tablespoonsful, in all, fresh thyme, rosemary and
mint, chopped
salt and pepper
oil

Heat a little oil and *sauté* onion and carrot for five
minutes then add liquid, herbs, salt and pepper and
simmer until vegetables are cooked.

Put mixture together with beans through a mincer (or
mash down beans and beat into mixture). Add egg and
sauce. Taste and adjust seasoning. Drop into shallow fat,
cook on both sides.

Method 1
To freeze: Cool thoroughly, wrap, label and freeze

Storage life: 2 months.

To thaw: Put frozen croquettes into hot fat.

Method 2
To freeze: Freeze mixture in shallow container.

Storage life: 2 months.

To thaw: Thaw for two hours at room temperature then
    cook as above.

Split Pea Burgers

100g (4 oz) split peas, cooked (see page 74)
1 small onion, chopped
1 tablespoonful whole barley flour
1 tablespoonful soya flour
1 cardamom seed, 3 mustard seeds, a tiny piece of
mace and small piece fresh ginger, all ground down in
a mortar (if not available add ground mace and pinch
ginger)
oil
salt and pepper
beaten egg and crumbs for coating

Sauté the onion in a little oil, adding the seasonings after a moment. When cooked, add split peas, which should not be too stiff. Mix well then add flours and cook until the mixture is stiff. Turn onto a wetted board and cool. Cut into pieces, shape, and egg and crumb (or use oat flakes). Either fry in deep hot fat, or shallow fat, when they will need turning after a few minutes.

Serve hot with a good sauce, such as tomato (page 111).

Method 1
To freeze: Freeze unshaped on flat board and wrap after freezing.

Storage life: 3 months.

To thaw: If thin, mixture can be cut while frozen, egg and crumbed then cooked immediately.

Method 2
To freeze: Transfer cooked burgers to freezer plate, wrap, label and freeze.

Storage life: 1 month.

To thaw: Put frozen into pan and heat thoroughly.

Lentil Bake

100g (4 oz) washed red lentils
1 small onion, chopped
1 large tomato, skinned and chopped
75g (3 oz) hard cheese, grated
1 tablespoonful oil
good pinch mustard
1 bay leaf
salt and pepper
boiling water

Sauté onions in oil for a few minutes, add tomato, bay leaf and lentils. Shake to cover lentils with oil and cook over gentle heat for a minute. Then add boiling water so that lentils are just covered. Stir, put lid on pan and cook for about 15 minutes on low heat, or until all the water is taken up and the lentils are soft.

Remove from heat, add seasonings and most of the cheese. Mix well and turn into greased dish. Sprinkle rest of cheese over top – this looks nice in lines to form a pattern. Bake in oven 200°C/400°F (Gas Mark 6) for half an hour. Best served hot with tomatoes.

To freeze: Prepare whole dish but do not bake. Simply cool and freeze. Use foil dish, freezer to oven dish or line dish with foil freeze in dish and them remove and wrap.

Storage life: 2 months.

To thaw: If wrapped in foil return to original greased dish and put into oven 200°C/400°F (Gas Mark 6) for 40 minutes or until cooked. If in dish lentil bake can either be put straight into the oven or allowed to thaw at room temperature for several hours.

*Mexican Beans

225g (8 oz) red kidney beans, soaked and cooked
4 large tomatoes, skinned and sliced
2 medium onions, skinned and chopped
2 cloves garlic, crushed
2 teaspoonsful vegetarian Worcester sauce
good pinch cayenne pepper
2 teaspoonsful paprika
pinch cinnamon and nutmeg
salt and pepper
275ml ($\frac{1}{2}$ pt) water
2 leaves fresh basil, chopped or a little dried
parsley
oil

Heat a little oil in a saucepan and *sauté* onion for five minutes. Add all the rest of the ingredients, mix well and bring to a simmer. Either simmer on low heat for half an hour or transfer all ingredients to casserole and cook in oven for one to two hours. (This is only economical if oven is already being used, so time will depend on heat of oven, but do not put in a very hot oven).

Serve with liberal sprinkling of chopped parsley and a good cooling drink!

To freeze: Cool quickly, freeze in rigid container.

Storage life: 1 month (or 3 months if you omit garlic.)

To thaw: Overnight at room temperature, then transfer to pan – add garlic if left out, bring to heat and simmer for ten minutes.

*Butter Bean Croquettes

225g (8 oz) butter beans, cooked and lightly drained
50g (2 oz) margarine
1 medium onion, chopped very finely
¼ small cauliflower, cooked, flourettes only
grated nutmeg
sprig fresh winter savoury chopped or a pinch of
dried sage
2 tablespoonsful tomato ketchup
salt and pepper

Melt margarine and *sauté* onion for five minutes. Mash butter beans with cauliflower then beat in onion and rest of the ingredients. Add extra liquid if needed (from butter beans) to make pliable consistency. Form into shapes having made sure it is sufficiently seasoned. An egg can be added if wished to help hold shape. Croquettes can be egg and crumbed, but this is not essential. Fry in shallow fat.

Method 1
To freeze: Cool thoroughly, wrap, label and freeze.

Storage life: 2 months.

To thaw: Heat frozen croquettes in hot fat.

Method 2
To freeze: Freeze mixture in flat shape for quick thawing.

Storage life: 2 months.

To thaw: Thaw for two hours at room temperature.

Method 3
To freeze: Freeze in croquettes before frying.

Storage life: 2 months.

To thaw: Egg and crumb frozen croquettes and then fry immediately or just put into pan from frozen.

*Soya Bean Stew

225g (8 oz) soya beans, cooked (see page 74)
50g (2 oz) sprouted chick peas
1 large onion, chopped
3 large tomatoes, skinned and chopped
450g (1 lb) french beans, chopped in 1-inch lengths
1 tablespoonful fresh thyme, milled
1 tablespoonful winter savory, milled
several sprigs parsley, milled
1 tablespoonful tomato *purée*
2 cloves garlic, crushed
salt and pepper
oil

Sauté the onion in a little oil for five minutes, then add the rest of the ingredients. If there is little water left from cooking the soya beans it may be necessary to add some. But do not make the mixture too wet. Bring to the boil, mixing all together then simmer for 15 to 20 minutes. Do not over-cook.

To freeze: Cool, transfer to a container and freeze.

Storage life: 1 month (or, if garlic is left out, 3 months.)

To thaw: Thaw in fridge overnight and then heat up gently in saucepan. Or put into a casserole in the oven to heat through. Add garlic at this stage if preferred.

This dish does well in a slow cooker. When all ingredients are mixed and heated, simply transfer to slow cooker on low for 5 to 6 hours.

*Treacle Field Beans

Field beans are very cheap, nutritious and tasty. This dish can be put into the bottom of the oven during a baking session and so will not need special cooking.

225g (8 oz) field beans, washed and soaked overnight
3 onions, sliced
2 carrots, diced
2 raw beetroot, diced
2 tablespoonsful black treacle
1 tablespoonful dark brown sugar
1½ level teaspoonsful dry mustard
small piece stick cinnamon
4 or 5 cloves
salt and fresh pepper
1 tablespoonful cider vinegar or lemon juice

Drain the beans, and put them in a casserole. Mix treacle, sugar, seasoning and spices with vinegar in a little hot water. Add vegetables to beans and mix them up. Stir water well, adding more if needed to combined ingredients. Pour water over beans and vegetables, making it up with more water to just cover. Put on a tight lid and cook in oven 170°C/325°F (Gas Mark 3) for 3 to 4 hours. Alternatively put at bottom of oven while cooking other things.

Can be cooked in a slow cooker on low for eight hours. Remove cloves and cinnamon.

Method 1
To Freeze: Cool and transfer to another container and freeze.

Storage life: 2 to 3 months.

To thaw: Thaw at room temperature for about 8 hours or overnight in fridge.

Method 2

To freeze: Freeze in casserole, then wrap and label (lining casserole with foil if wished).

Storage life: 2 to 3 months.

To thaw: Reheat from frozen in oven at 190°C/375°F (Gas Mark 5) for about 1½ hours.

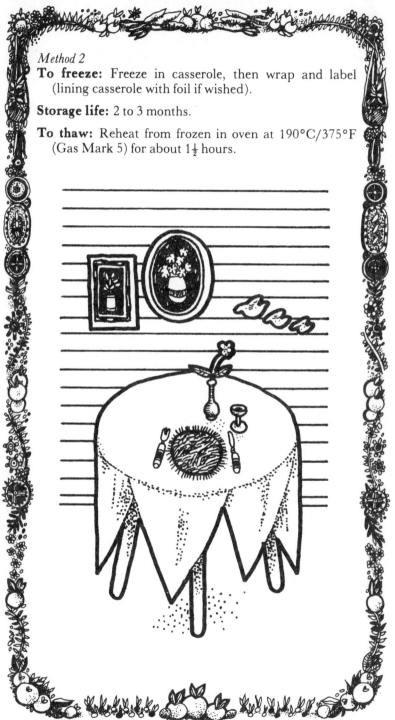

10
NUTS

*Hazel Wheat Roll

100g (4 oz) hazelnuts, chopped and roasted
50g (2 oz) sprouted wheat (see page 157)
75g (3 oz) pineapple chunks, chopped
rough puff pastry made with 100 per cent flour

Make the pastry (page 41) and allow it to rest in the refrigerator or a cold place for half an hour. Then roll it out to an oblong about 6 ins x 12 ins. Leaving long edges free spread the mixed nuts, wheat and pineapple over pastry. Damp the edges and roll up like a swiss roll.

Transfer to a baking sheet and flatten slightly to an oval section, then cut diagonally along the top of the roll. Glaze the top with soya milk, or egg. Bake in oven 230°C/450°F (Gas Mark 8) for 20 to 25 minutes. Serve hot or cold.

To freeze: Cool, open freeze and then wrap or prepare to stage when roll is ready for glazing. Freeze and wrap.

Storage life: 2 months.

To thaw: Thaw overnight in fridge, or for shorter time at room temperature. Or put straight into oven as above allowing extra time if roll was frozen raw. Cover top if necessary to avoid burning.

*Hazel Nut Balls in Curry Sauce

225g (8 oz) hazel nuts, ground
50g (2 oz) brown bread, soaked in water and
squeezed out
a small piece turnip, chopped small
1 medium-sized carrot, chopped small
1 medium-sized onion, chopped small
oil
¼ teaspoonful each of ground ginger, cinnamon,
nutmeg, ground cloves, black pepper
salt
curry sauce

Sauté onion, turnip and carrot in a little oil with spices
and seasoning until onion becomes transparent and
vegetables are soft. (This can be hastened by addition of
a little water) be sure not to burn. Mash this down to a
purée, then add nuts and bread. Mix well and form into
balls.

An egg can be used to help the mixture to adhere. At
this stage you can egg and crumb or just roll balls in
breadcrumbs or oatflakes. Set nutballs aside in
refrigerator.

Make the sauce. Then fry the nut balls and serve hot
with the sauce.

To freeze: Nutballs can be frozen before or after frying,
   although it is better to freeze before, as, in any case,
   they need to be cooked again. Freeze sauce separately.
   (See section on sauces.)

Storage life: 2 to 3 months.

To thaw: Thaw out first or fry from frozen or nutballs
   can be cooked in oven from frozen.
   N.B. Do not egg and crumb before freezing.

*Hazelnut and Cashew Savoury

350g (12 oz) mixed hazel and cashew nuts, ground
50g (2 oz) bread crumbs
50g (2 oz) millet flakes
50g (2 oz) oat flakes
2 onions, chopped finely
a small piece of turnip, grated
2 tablespoonsful tomato *purée*
1 tablespoonful yeast extract
large sprig parsley and thyme, milled
a few leaves fresh mint and sage, milled
grate of nutmeg
bay leaf
good dash tabasco or other strong sauce
salt and pepper
oil
water

Heat the oil and *sauté* onions and turnip with the bay leaf for about seven minutes. Mix the dry ingredients, then add all the rest (removing the bay leaf). Add enough water to make a stiff dropping consistency.

Grease a 2 lb loaf tin or two smaller ones. Pack the mixture in and bake in oven 200°C/400°F (Gas Mark 6) for an hour in smaller tins and 1½ hours for the large one.

Turn out and serve hot with sauce and vegetables or cold with salad.

To freeze: Line tin with foil before baking. Cool, freeze in tin then remove tin and wrap.

Storage life: 2 months.

To thaw: To eat cold, wrap and either leave in refrigerator overnight or at room temperature for 4 to 5 hours.

To serve hot, unwrap and return to original greased tin, heat in oven 180°C/350°F (Gas Mark 4) for an hour or until heated right through. It is better to leave to thaw for an hour or two once you have returned to the tin.

*Nut Savoury Mixture

350g (12 oz) mixed nuts, ground fine
50g (2 oz) oat, millet or barley flakes
100g (4 oz) brown bread
1 large onion, finely chopped
25g (1 oz) soya flour
2 tablespoonsful tomato *purée*
good dash tabasco or other strong sauce
25g (1 oz) oil or margarine
1 teaspoonful yeast extract
¼ teaspoonful nutmeg, freshly grated
¼ teaspoonful mace
big handful of fresh herbs, for instance: large sprig
parsley, small sprig rosemary, a little marjoram and
mint. Use small quantity of dry herbs if no fresh
available
salt and pepper
water

Simmer onion in the fat until it is soft. Meanwhile soak the bread in some water, then fork it into pieces. Add all the ingredients, mincing the herbs and using enough water to make a fairly stiff consistency.

Leave for five minutes and then stir again adding more water if needed. Put into a very well greased loaf tin. Bake in a hot oven 200°C/400°F (Gas Mark 6) for 45 minutes. Then turn out and return to oven after basting with oil. Bake for further ten minutes.

Serve with a good sauce, roast or jacket potatoes and a green vegetable. It can also be served cold with salad.

Method 1

To freeze: Line baking tin with foil. Cool, freeze then remove from tin, pack and label.

Storage life: 2 to 3 months.

To thaw: To serve cold, keep in fridge overnight and bring out to room temperature 2-3 hours before serving. To serve hot return to container and either thaw first or put straight into moderate oven until heated right through.

Method 2

To freeze: Freeze as above before cooking.

Storage life: 2 to 3 months.

To thaw: Remove all wrapping and put into original tin which has been well greased. Cook from frozen allowing extra half an hour. Check that it is cooked right through.

Method 3

To freeze: Freeze the mixture uncooked in a container.

Storage life: 2 to 3 months.

To thaw: Thaw at room temperature for 4-5 hours, or overnight in fridge. Then use as wished.

Russian Nutburgers

225g (8 oz) mixed nuts, ground
1 large carrot, finely grated
1 large onion, finely chopped
2 tablespoonsful capers, finely chopped (or use
nasturtium seeds)
1 tablespoonful soya flour
225g (8 oz) mashed cooked potatoes
1 tablespoonful parsley, chopped
2 egg yolks
4 tablespoonsful sour cream, or yogurt
salt and pepper
oil for frying

Mix all ingredients together to a workable consistency.
With floured hands form into flat round shapes and fry in
hot fat.

Method 1
To freeze: Cool the cooked burgers and freeze on a flat
   plate, separating layers with film or foil.

Storage life: 3 months.

To thaw: Heat frozen burgers in hot fat until heated
   right through.

Method 2
To freeze: Freeze mixture in mass or as shaped burgers.

Storage life: 3 months.

To thaw: Stand at room temperature for two hours if
   unshaped, otherwise put frozen, uncooked burgers
   straight into hot fat and cook.

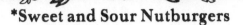

*Sweet and Sour Nutburgers

8 nutburgers using nut savoury recipe, or thick slices
of a tinned nut savoury
1 small onion, sliced
1 medium carrot, cut into 1-inch strips
1 tablespoonful 100 per cent flour
4 fresh apricots, halved and stoned
2 tablespoonsful oil
150ml (¼ pt) water
2 tablespoonsful lemon juice
2 teaspoonsful dark brown sugar
2 teaspoonsful soya sauce
salt and pepper

Cook the burgers until nicely browned and then put
aside, keeping them hot. Add onion and carrot to the pan
and cook, stirring. Blend flour with a little water, and
then stir in the rest. Add this to onions and carrots,
stirring. Add remaining ingredients except apricots and
burgers. Simmer for five minutes then add apricots and
cook for a further five minutes. Serve with the hot
nutburgers.

Alternatively, all ingredients can be put into a
casserole once the flour has been blended in and cooked.
Put casserole into a medium oven for half an hour.

To freeze: Prepare in freezer container, or line casserole
with foil, leave to cool and freeze. Remove casserole,
pack, label and freeze.

Storage life: 3 months

To thaw: Stand at room temperature for three hours or
in fridge overnight, then heat gently in a saucepan, or
oven.

Alternatively, put straight into medium oven from
freezer and leave for one hour or until heated right
through.

Frozen apricots can be used for this dish. They can be
put straight into saucepan in their frozen state before
adding burgers. Allow extra ten minutes cooking time.

Vegetarian Moussaka

450g (1 lb) aubergines, sliced
175g (6 oz) cashew nuts, coarsely grated
2 large onions, chopped
1 large carrot, coarsely grated
1 clove garlic, crushed
1l (1¼ pts) tomato sauce (see page 111)
1 tablespoonful parsley, chopped
salt and pepper
oil

Topping:
100g (4 oz) hard cheese, grated
1 tablespoonful parmesan cheese
1 egg, lightly beaten
2 tablespoonsful top of milk

Sauté the onion and garlic in a little oil for five minutes. Remove these draining as much oil as possible, then fry the sliced aubergine.

Place into a greased casserole layering onions, carrots, aubergines, and nuts. Season as required. Pour over the hot tomato sauce. Put into a moderate oven 180°C/350°F (Gas Mark 4) for 30 minutes. Combine all topping ingredients, and add to top of casserole. Return to oven and cook until top is lightly cooked. Serve sprinkled with parsley.

To freeze: Prepare for oven but do not cook. Line casserole with foil if prepared and remove when moussaka is frozen then wrap and label. Grated cheese can be frozen separately.

Storage life: 2 to 3 months.

To thaw: Remove from wrapping and replace in greased casserole. Thaw overnight in fridge with top covered, or for several hours at room temperature. Cook in oven as above and follow recipes. Moussaka can be put straight into the oven from frozen, but allow an extra hour, and it is a good idea to check after half an hour and gently break up ingredients, to hasten heating.

11
RICE AND WHOLEGRAINS

*Rice and Walnut Gratin

225g (8 oz) wholegrain long rice
100g (4 oz) walnuts, finely chopped, reserving 4
large
225g (8 oz) tomatoes, sliced thinly
4 tablespoonsful fresh brown breadcrumbs
1 bay leaf
salt and pepper
parsley
sauce, such as tomato or mushroom (see page 111)

Cook rice with the bay leaf in $2\frac{1}{2}$ times quantity of water. Remove bayleaf and add salt and pepper.

Grease four individual dishes and layer in the rice, nuts and tomatoes in that order. Sprinkle breadcrumbs on top and heat under grill. Serve garnished with chopped parsley and one whole walnut each with sauce hot.

To freeze: Freeze cooked rice (well drained and dry) and nuts chopped ready in separate containers. Breadcrumbs can also be ready and all put into one polythene bag with sauce, labelled, 'ready to use'.

Storage Life: 1 month.

To thaw: Heat rice in double steamer, gently heat sauce in a pan. Then follow recipe. All ingredients can be taken out of freezer and left at room temperature for about two hours before use.

*Brazil Nut Pilaf

1 cupful uncooked whole rice
50g (2 oz) brazil nuts, sliced
50g (2 oz) margarine
1 small onion, chopped
3 sticks celery, chopped
2 cubes vegetarian bouillon
2½ cupsful water
¼ teaspoonful salt

Sauté the onion and celery in the margarine for five minutes. Add the rice, shake and cook for a few minutes stirring to mix. Bring water to the boil and stir into the mixture, add bouillon, salt and nuts. Cover and simmer for about 30 minutes or until rice is cooked.

To freeze: Allow to cool and then freeze in a flat container. (Make sure rice is cooked and dry).

Storage life: 1 month.

To thaw: Thaw overnight in container in refrigerator, or an hour at room temperature, then put a little margarine into a saucepan, heat, and add pilaf, shaking and stirring gently to heat through.

*Paprika Pilaf

Recipe as for Brazil Nut Pilaf but with the following differences. Add a small diced red pepper when cooking onions and a heaped teaspoonful of paprika. Omit brazil nuts and instead use slivered almonds. Do not include in cooking, but toast almonds under the grill and sprinkle over pilaf when serving.

Freeze, store and thaw as Brazil Pilaf, but store nuts separately.

Mushroom Whole Grain Flan

Crust:
100g (4 oz) 100 per cent wholewheat flour
25g (1 oz) millet flakes
25g (1 oz) oat flakes
25g (1 oz) rye flakes
25g (1 oz) barley flakes
75g (3 oz) margarine or white nut fat
sprig thyme and parsley, chopped
salt and pepper

Filling:
1 small onion, chopped
2 tomatoes, sliced
2 eggs
150ml ($\frac{1}{4}$ pt) milk
100g (4 oz) mushrooms sliced
grate of nutmeg
salt and pepper

Make crust by mixing all the crust ingredients, rubbing fat in with fingertips. Press mixture into a deep sided flan tin. Bake blind in oven 200°C/400°F (Gas Mark 6) for 10 minutes. Lay tomatoes, onion and mushrooms on the hot flan. Cover with rest of ingredients whisked together. Return to oven and cook for 1 hour. Serve hot or cold.

Method 1

To freeze: When flan comes out of oven cool completely, open freeze and then wrap closely.

Storage life: 1 month.

To thaw: Leave overnight in fridge. To serve cold, bring out to room temperature 1 hour before serving. To serve hot, put in oven at 180°C/350°F (Gas Mark 4) with covered top for 20 minutes. If it is in a suitable container it can be put straight in oven from freezer.

Method 2

To freeze: Add tomatoes, onions and mushrooms to baked flan case. Cool and freeze.

Storage life: 2 months.

To thaw: Remove from wrapping and continue recipe, allowing an extra five minutes cooking time.

*Savoury Whole Grain Flan

Crust:
100g (4 oz) 100 per cent wholewheat flour
25g (1 oz) millet flakes
25g (1 oz) oat flakes
25g (1 oz) rye flour
25g (1 oz) barley flakes
75g (3 oz) margarine or white nut fat
1 dessertspoonful yeast extract
sprig parsley, chopped
salt and pepper

Filling:
400g (14 oz) tin of tomatoes
50g (2 oz) almonds, chopped
1 large onion, chopped
50g (2 oz) soya protein, flavourless mince
1 tablespoonful tomato *purée*
½ vegetarian bouillon
2 leaves fresh basil, chopped or a pinch of dried
salt and pepper
oil

Make crust by mixing all crust ingredients, rubbing fat in with fingertips. Press mixture into a large flan ring or two small ones. Bake blind in oven at 200°C/400°F (Gas Mark 6) for ten minutes.

Prepare filling by *sautéeing* onion in oil for five minutes. Add tomatoes, bouillon, *purée* and seasoning and stir for two or three minutes. Add soya protein and mix well. Pour onto flan case, sprinkle nuts on top, return to oven at 190°C/375°F (Gas Mark 5) for 20 minutes. Best served hot.

Method 1
To freeze: Cool and freeze cooked flan (open freeze, remove flan ring but leave base, then wrap and label.)

Storage life: 2 months.

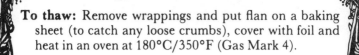

To thaw: Remove wrappings and put flan on a baking sheet (to catch any loose crumbs), cover with foil and heat in an oven at 180°C/350°F (Gas Mark 4).

Method 2
To freeze: Prepare to final stage then open freeze as above.

Storage life: 2 months.

To thaw: Return ring carefully and put straight into oven at 190°C/375°F (Gas Mark 5) for 40 minutes or until cooked.

Method 3
To freeze: Freeze prepared crust mixture in a polythene bag.

Storage life: 3 months.

To thaw: Press mixture straight onto flan ring and continue as recipe.

*Stuffed Peppers

4 ripe medium sized peppers (red ones are sweeter)
100g (4 oz) wholegrain long rice
50g (2 oz) mushrooms, cleaned and chopped
25g (1 oz) whole green lentils
50g (2 oz) sprouted wheat (3 days)
2 large tomatoes, skinned and chopped
½ chili, chopped fine
1 clove garlic, crushed
salt and pepper
oil

Cook the rice and lentils in boiling water until cooked but firm. Meanwhile fry the mushrooms in a little oil. Combine all ingredients. Mix well and simmer over a very gentle heat for a moment. Add water if necessary to make a slack mixture. Taste for seasoning and adjust.

While rice is cooking cut a small lid in the peppers and scoop out the seeds. Plunge whole peppers into boiling water and simmer for five minutes. Remove carefully and drain, standing them upside down to retain their shape.

Grease a dish in which the peppers can stand up supporting each other. Fill peppers and put in the dish. Put the lids back on the peppers and cover with lightly buttered foil. Bake in oven at 180°C/350°F (Gas Mark 4) for 30 minutes.

To freeze: Cool and then open freeze, then wrap peppers separately. Alternatively, freeze uncooked, wrapping individually when peppers are frozen.

Storage life: 2 months (longer if garlic is omitted).

To thaw: Unwrap and return to greased dish. Cook as above allowing extra 20 minutes if they are frozen uncooked.

12

PANCAKES AND PASTA

*Pizza

Pizza is such an easy thing to make, and yet because there are so many possible toppings it is a versatile and tasty meal. Use either the bread dough recipe (page 118) or the plain scone recipe (page 120).

When making bread I nearly always take enough out of the dough to make a pizza. Set it aside in a plastic bag to rise once. Then knock it down and knead for a few moments. Put it on to a greased plate and work it from the centre towards the edges. Turn the edges up slightly, brush lightly with oil and then put back in the plastic bag for about ten minutes. When it has risen put on the topping.

Obvious toppings are sliced or drained tinned tomatoes, thinly sliced onions, olives, grated cheese of different varieties and strips of red and green pepper. You can also use nasturtium seeds, sunflower seeds, tahina, strips of cooked dried apricots or prunes.

Whichever you use make sure that the pizza is not soggy before cooking, and yet you have to guard against the topping drying up. A good layer of cheese or some moist tomatoes on top will prevent drying. Bake in oven 200-220°C/400-425°F (Gas Mark 6) for about 15 minutes.

To freeze: Freeze either cooked or uncooked.

Storage life: 3 months.

To thaw: Allow time at room temperature or put straight into the oven for ten minutes.

Pancakes

**75g (3 oz) 100 per cent wholewheat flour with the
bran sifted out
1 level tablespoonful soya flour
3 tablespoonsful milk
2 large eggs
milk
pinch of salt**

Sift the flours together (use the bran for something else) and add the salt. Make a well in the centre, add eggs and the three tablespoonsful of milk. Whisk these together with small whisk or fork, gradually incorporating flour from the sides. Add more milk as mixture becomes too dry, but beat well all the time and aim to achieve a smooth mixture before adding much more milk. Set aside in the refrigerator for half an hour or more.

Heat a little oil in a good frying pan. Make sure pancake batter is of a thin consistency. Pour off any excess oil from the pan and pour in a little batter. Cook on moderate heat, turning carefully to cook both sides. The first one or two may not be very even, but you should get into a rhythm and be able to judge how hot the pan needs to be and how much fat to add. In fact, you will need very little.

As the pancakes are cooked pile them up with foil or waxed paper between each.

To freeze: Cool completely and carefully wrap.

Storage life: 2 months.

To thaw: Leave in package at room temperature for several hours, or separate each pancake and they will thaw very quickly. Either heat over hot water on a plate and then fill, or fill first and heat in a low oven.

Pancakes can form the basis of many savoury dishes, and so it is very useful to have a supply in the freezer. The following recipe can be used for savoury or sweet dishes. 81 per cent flour will give a lighter result, but the 100 per cent flour tastes better.

Pancake Pudding

12 very small pancakes (see page 100)
225g (8 oz) field beans or kidney beans
275ml (¼ pt) tomato sauce (see page 111)
50g (2 oz) grated cheese

Line a foil pudding basin with some of the pancakes. Add the cooked beans to the sauce and season if needed. Layer beans with rest of pancakes, leaving enough to cover the top. Cover top well with overlapping pancakes. Sprinkle the cheese over and put into a moderate oven, 190°C/375°F (Gas Mark 5) for about 30 minutes to heat through. Turn out carefully and serve with green beans or a side salad.

To freeze: Freeze in basin before cooking.

Storage life: 2 to 3 months.

To thaw: Put frozen into oven as above but give an extra 20 minutes or thaw overnight in fridge or at room temperature before baking.

Spinach Ravioli

225g (8 oz) flour (use sieved 100 per cent or 81 per cent)
15g (½ oz) margarine
1 egg, beaten. Retain a little and mix this with some water
¼ teaspoonful of salt

Filling:
225g (8 oz) cooked and well drained spinach
1 hard boiled egg, chopped
50g (2 oz) cashew nuts, ground
1 teaspoonful tomato *purée*
salt and pepper

Rub fat and flour, add salt, make a stiff paste with the egg, adding very little water if essential. Put into fridge for 15 minutes.

Roll out very thinly on well floured board and leave to stand for five to ten minutes before cutting. Then cut into rings with a fluted cutter.

Place a little filling in middle of each. Damp edges with the reserved egg and water. Fold over and seal very well. Poach for about ten minutes in salted boiling water. Drain, keep hot in a dish. When all are cooked sprinkle with a little parmesan cheese, pour over a tomato sauce (see page 111) and brown under the grill. To make the filling simply mix all ingredients together.

Method 1
To freeze: Ravioli can be frozen cooked, without sauce.

Storage life: 2 to 3 months.

To thaw: Thaw at room temperature or in fridge, then continue with recipe.

Method 2
To freeze: Freeze before poaching.

Storage life: 2 to 3 months.

To thaw: Poach from frozen, making sure water comes quickly back to boiling. Give longer time to cook.

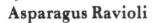

Asparagus Ravioli

Ravioli made as in recipe for spinach ravioli

1 small tin asparagus
2 small eggs
50g (2 oz) cashew nuts, ground
salt and pepper
a little milk

Beat the eggs with just a little milk and some salt and pepper, and scramble with a little margarine in a pan. Mix in the chopped, drained asparagus and the cashew nuts. Check on seasoning and proceed as for spinach ravioli.

Serve with a cheese, tomato or asparagus sauce. (Make the latter using the liquid from the asparagus.)

Method 1
To freeze: Freeze cooked but without the sauce.

Storage life: 2 to 3 months.

To thaw: Thaw at room temperature, or longer in fridge, then continue with recipe.

Method 2
To freeze: Freeze before poaching.

Storage life: 2 to 3 months.

To thaw: Poach from frozen, making sure that the water comes quickly back to boiling and give longer time.

Nut and Paté Ravioli

Ravioli made as in previous ravioli recipe (page 102)
50g (2 oz) cashew nuts, ground
2 eggs, hard boiled, finely chopped
1 small tin bought vegetarian *paté*
rind and juice of half a lemon, thinly grated
salt and pepper

Make sure that the eggs are well mixed and then mash in the *paté*. Add ground cashew nuts, lemon rind and juice. Season and use to fill ravioli. Serve with tomato sauce.

To freeze: As for ravioli in previous recipe.

Storage life: 1 month.

To thaw: As in other ravioli recipes.

Cannelloni in Tomato Sauce

This is a tasty recipe using nut, savoury or lentil mixtures as filling or the ingredients given below.

Large (1-inch) cannelloni, preferably wholegrain
100g (4 oz) lemon and thyme stuffing
50g (2 oz) bought vegetarian 'sausage' mixture
50g (2 oz) hazel nuts, ground
fresh lemon balm, thyme and parsley, minced
water

Put all the ingredients into a bowl and mix well. Cover with boiling water and stir, make this a fairly dropping consistency. Leave for five minutes. It should then have stiffened up a little and be a good piping consistency. Transfer the mixture to a piping bag.

Grease a long deep dish. Pipe the mixture into the cannelloni and place side by side in the dish. Cover with tomato sauce (see page 111). Make sure that the cannelloni are completely covered. Sprinkle a few grated nuts on top and dot with butter or margarine. Cook in oven 190°C/375°F (Gas Mark 5) for 30 minutes.

To freeze: Cool and freeze in the dish or line dish with foil and then remove when food is frozen.

The cannelloni will freeze raw, but they do tend to split. This does not affect the taste.

Storage life: 3 months.

To thaw: Put frozen dish straight into a moderate oven, covering to prevent burning, and cook for an hour.

Stuffed Lasagne

Use wholegrain lasagne and cook in boiling water for five minutes. Drain and cool. Shape the stuffing mixture into sausage shapes and wind the lasagne round like a bandage. Proceed as above recipe.

13
SAUCES AND SOUPS

A good home-made sauce can make all the difference to a dish, but in the last minute rush to get a family meal to the table it is very easy to give up on the sauces! This is where the freezer can play a part. A roux can be frozen in small amounts providing a good basis for a quick sauce.

*Basic Roux

**225g (8 oz) margarine
350g (12 oz) 100 per cent flour with the bran sieved
out**

Melt the margarine carefully in a saucepan. When it is completely melted beat in half the flour, return to the heat turned very low and gradually beat in as much flour as the mixture will take to form a good consistency that is not too dry, but not at all fatty. Stir for about 2 minutes when this stage is reached then take off the heat and cool. Freeze in useable amounts. This can be easily done by putting heaped tablespoonsful on to foil and packing them individually into a small container. Wrap and freeze. These will last for 3 months or longer. To use, put frozen into the liquid to be thickened for a sauce, and stir very well over heat. Or put with liquid and flavouring straight into a liquidizer for a few seconds, then stir over heat until sauce thickens.

*Basic Béchamel

Another method is to make a very thick béchamel sauce, and then use this as a basis for a variety of different sauces.

To 275ml (½ pt) of milk (plant milk can be used) add 1 medium carrot cut small, 1 small, chopped onion, a small piece of celery chopped, a piece of mace, 1 bay leaf and about 6 peppercorns. Bring the milk gently to the boil, and then infuse for half an hour. Meanwhile make a roux with 75g (3 oz) margarine and about 100g (4 oz) 100 per cent flour, cook a little as above when the right consistency is obtained. Strain the milk and use this to make a very thick sauce. Stir well, adding a little liquid if needed (milk or water) then cool, and divide into three portions and freeze. Each portion will be enough to make a sauce using about 275ml (½ pt) of liquid. You can store for about three months.

The way this basic béchamel is used depends on the kind of sauce that is being made.

Cheese Sauce

Basic béchamel, frozen
100g (4 oz) hard cheese, grated
1 teaspoonful mustard, dry
275ml (½ pt) milk

Warm the milk to below boiling point. Put béchamel into blender, add the milk and cheese and mustard (rubbed into the cheese) and blend for a minute. Put in saucepan and gently bring to boiling point, whisking with a balloon whisk. Taste and season if needed.

*Caper Sauce

Basic béchamel, frozen
2 tablespoonsful capers, chopped or use nasturtium
seeds either straight from the plant or when they
have been marinated in cider vinegar.
Under 275ml (½ pt) milk

Heat the milk, put the capers and béchamel into the blender, pour in about three-quarters of the milk and blend. Put in a saucepan and bring to boil whisking. Add more milk if the sauce is too thick. Taste and season if needed.

*Parsley Sauce

Use parsley, fresh or frozen and proceed as for caper sauce.

*Onion Sauce

**basic béchamel sauce, frozen
225g (8 oz) onions,** *sautéed* **until soft in a little
margarine**

Proceed as for caper sauce.

*Quick Curry Sauce

**Onion sauce made with basic béchamel
1 dessertspoonful curry paste
1 teaspoonful garam masala
pinch of coriander, cardamom and paprika**

Add spices to onion sauce in a blender.

Better still take a variety of seeds and spices and grind down in a mortar. e.g. a few mustard seeds, one or two coriander seeds, a little mace, small piece of cinnamon. Experiment with caution to begin with as some of these are very strong indeed. The taste is much more fresh than using curry powder.

From the foregoing it is obvious that any variety of sauce can be made very quickly once you have prepared the basic foundation. Try varieties or single herbs, obvious ones being parsley, sorrel, fennel; and combinations like thyme, rosemary, marjoram, curry plant and so on.

*Tomato Sauce

**400g (14 oz) tin of tomatoes or equivalent fresh,
skinned and chopped
1 large onion, finely chopped
25g (1 oz) margarine
25g (1 oz) 100 per cent flour with bran sieved out
1 teaspoonful dark brown sugar
grated peel of half a lemon
bay leaf
3 or 4 cloves
handful fresh herbs to include thyme, lemon balm,
marjoram, and a little mint. Dried herbs are not the
same, but of course frozen herbs can be used
salt and pepper
water
a little red wine or apple juice**

Melt fat in saucepan, add onion and cook for five
minutes, add flour, stir well and cook for further two to
three minutes. Add tomatoes and all other ingredients
except water and wine. Stir on a low heat. Add a little
water, increasing the amount as neeeded for the
thickness required. Simmer for 20 minutes. Remove bay
leaf and cloves.

The sauce is very good left like this. It may be blended
to a smooth finish in an electric blender or put through a
sieve. Just before serving increase heat for a moment
stirring and add wine or juice. Test for taste and add
seasoning if required.

To freeze: Add as little liquid as possible while cooking
the sauce. Freeze when cold in small quantities (having
removed bay leaf and cloves). If very concentrated
freeze in ice cube containers and then transfer to bags
or boxes.

Storage life: 12 months.

To thaw: Put small cubes straight in soups or stews,
gently heat sauce from frozen in a saucepan which has
a little boiling water in first or stand at room
temperature for an hour or two.

Soups

Soups can be as nourishing as you wish. They are a good way of making the best use of outside leaves, tough parts of vegetables and so on.

All soups can be frozen, but there is no point in taking up freezer space with a lot of frozen water! So soups should be as concentrated as possible and not highly seasoned. It is only sensible to freeze vegetables in soup form when you have a surplus, when you want to prepare well in advance for a special occasion or when it is convenient to make double quantities and the excess can be frozen.

Soups take a long time to thaw, but once thawing has started they can be gently heated through in a saucepan, or in a double boiler, or even in a suitable container in the oven if there is space while other things are being baked.

Garnishes

Small quantities of croûtons can be stored ready fried but do not keep for more than two months.

Toast melba can be prepared and frozen and used straight from the freezer. Toast thin slices of bread, then carefully slice through again and gently toast cut side so that it curls up. Do not use new bread. Store in a rigid container in the freezer.

Julienne vegetables can be stored already cut up and mixed, then they can be put straight from frozen into the soup 5 minutes before serving. Cut vegetables into very thin short sticks, freeze without blanching. Store for one to two months.

Sprouted seeds, grains and beans can also be frozen for one to two months and added to soups three minutes before serving. Most suitable are wheat, fenugreek, chick peas, lentils. Freeze after four days sprouting.

Grated cheese can be stored in a container and a few tablespoonsful sprinkled on soup immediately before serving.

Borsch

**2 large raw beetroots, chopped
1 medium onion, chopped
2 sticks celery, finely chopped
1 clove garlic
½ lemon, juiced
550ml (1 pt) water
sherry
grate of nutmeg
sour cream or yogurt can be used
salt and pepper**

Put all ingredients, except sherry, sour cream and nutmeg into a pan, season only a little. Bring to boil and simmer gently for 30 minutes.

Put through a *mouli-sieve*. Return to saucepan, add a little sherry and a grate of nutmeg, taste and season if needed. Serve hot with sour cream or yogurt served separately.

To freeze: After sieving cool and freeze.

Storage life: 3 months.

To thaw: Thaw in fridge overnight, can be served cold. When serving, hot soup can be thawed a little and then gently heated from cold. Check seasoning and serve as above.

*Pea Pod Soup

**1kg (about 2 lbs) new peas
225g (8 oz) new carrots, chopped
1 onion, chopped
large handful fresh mint
good sprig parsley
salt and pepper
2 tablespoonsful soya flour
water**

Pod the peas and put them aside for use in some other way. Make sure the pea pods are well washed, then put them in a pan with all the rest of the ingredients except the soya flour with enough water to cover. Bring to the boil and simmer until all the vegetables are cooked, and the flesh can be easily scraped from the pods.

Put all the ingredients through a *mouli-sieve*. Mix the soya flour with a little water and then add some of the vegetable liquid stirring to make a smooth cream. Return the liquid and soya cream to the saucepan and bring back to the boil stirring. Add more water if it will take it, but this soup is best fairly thick.

To make it thicker a potato can be included in the ingredients or a tablespoonful of plain flour can be added at the same time as the soya flour.

To freeze: Cool and freeze in as concentrated form as possible.

Storage life: 4 months.

To thaw: Leave overnight in fridge or stand out at room temperature for some time and then gently heat in pan.

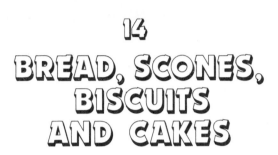

14

BREAD, SCONES, BISCUITS AND CAKES

Basic Sweet Dough

450g (1 lb) 100 per cent flour with bran sifted out
25g (1 oz) soya flour
15g (½ oz) fresh yeast or half the amount if dried
yeast
75g (3 oz) butter or margarine
25g (1 oz) soft brown sugar
1 egg, beaten
½ teaspoonful salt
275 ml (½ pt) milk and water mixed

Rub fat into the sifted flours, sugar and salt. Set bowl in
a warm place. Cream yeast with a little warm milk, then
stir in rest of milk and water. (If using dried yeast pour a
little hand hot water over and stir in a teaspoonful of
sugar, leave until frothy).

Beat egg into yeast mixture and then make a well in
the centre of the flour, pour in liquid and mix very well.
This dough is more sticky than normal bread dough. If it
gets too sticky to handle add a little flour, but not enough
to make it dry. Set aside in oiled bowl and cover with a
polythene bag to double in bulk.

Remarks about rising in basic bread dough apply
here. Use this dough for a variety of buns, and sweet
breads.

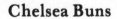

Chelsea Buns

After first rising, knock down the dough and then roll it out gently on a floured board to make a rectangle. Mix together 75g (3 oz) currants, 25g (1 oz) mixed peel and 1 teaspoonful of mixed spice. Sprinkle these on the dough then damp the edges and roll up. Cut into 1-inch slices and set to rise on a greased baking sheet. When they are well risen – in about 20 minutes – bake in a hot oven, 230°C/450°F (Gas Mark 8) for 20 minutes. Take them out, brush with water and then sprinkle with a little demerara sugar, return to the oven for a few minutes.

Bubble Tea Bread

This makes an unusual and delicious sweet bread. Follow the recipe for sweet dough until the first rising, then knock the dough down and divide into three pieces. Have ready 2 1 lb (450g) loaf tins or sponge cake tins and prepare the following three dishes while the bread is rising.

1. 1 tablespoonful cinnamon and 2 tablespoonsful soft brown sugar, well mixed.
2. 2 tablespoonsful coarsely ground almonds (with skins still on) and 2 tablespoonsful dark brown sugar.
3. 2 tablespoonsful poppy seeds and 2 tablespoonsful dark sugar.

Melt some butter or margarine. Divide each of the three pieces of dough into small balls. They do not need to be even sized. Brush the dough balls with melted fat and dip into one of the prepared mixtures, then into a tin. Vary the flavours so that each loaf has the different balls fairly evenly distributed. Leave to rise for about half an hour and then bake in a hot oven 220°C/425°F (Gas Mark 7) for about 30 minutes.

These can be glazed with sugar boiled in water for two minutes – a tablespoonful brown sugar to a tablespoonful water.

Yeast Tea Ring

Follow the recipe to the first rising, then knead to a smooth dough and divide in two. Roll each out to a rectangle about 4 ins (10cm) wide and 1 ft (30.5cm) long. Mix about 75g (3 oz) ground almonds with three tablespoonsful of warmed honey and spread on the centre of the rectangle. Finely chop about four dried apricots and sprinkle on one tea ring. Sprinkle some raisins, chopped date or small pieces of apple on the other rectangle.

Roll both rings up joining into a circle, damp edges with water to help join. Put them on to a greased baking tray and leave to rise for 15 to 20 minutes. Bake in hot oven 230°C/450°F (Gas Mark 8) for 20 to 25 minutes.

These can be iced, or a little honey spread over the tops – sticky, but tasty! These freeze well but do not put icing or honey on before freezing.

Thumb Buns

Follow the sweet dough recipe to the first raising. Knead for a few minutes on a floured board, and then divide the dough into convenient sized buns. Set these on a greased baking sheet leaving plenty of space in between. With a floured thumb press a well into the centre of each bun making a good hole. Fill the hole with a tasty filling. It could just be home-made strawberry or raspberry jam or one of the following:

1. Ground poppy seeds with honey.
2. Finely chopped dried apricots with honey.
3. Grounds nuts with a little sugar and a flavouring such as vanilla or cinnamon.
4. Chopped dates and apple with honey.

Allow the buns to rise for about 20 minutes and then bake in oven at 220°C/425°F (Gas Mark 7) for 15 to 20 minutes.

You can pinch the top back over the filling, brush with cold milk and sprinkle with a little sugar.

*Basic Loaf Recipe

1.35kg (3 lb) 100 per cent wholewheat flour
50g (2 oz) soya flour
25g (1 oz) dried yeast *or*
50g (2 oz) fresh yeast
850ml (1½ pt) water
1 tablespoonful dark brown sugar
1 dessertspoonful salt
25g (1 oz) butter, margarine or oil

Sieve the flours and salt into a bowl (replace bran) and set in a warm place. Heat the water to hand hot, put a little into a small basin, and add yeast and sugar. Cream fresh yeast and stir in dried yeast, leave for seven to ten minutes, or until the liquid is well frothed up. About half fill the bowl with water.

If using fat rub this in to the flours. Oil can be added at the same time as the liquid. Oil the tins. (This amount is enough for 2 1 lb (450g) tins and 1 2 lb (900g) tin). Put tins to warm. Add the yeast to flour mixture, gradually adding the rest of the water as you work it in to the flour. Take care not to add too much. (Flours vary in the amount of water that they take up.) The dough should leave the sides of the bowl clean when it is the right texture. Knead with a pushing movement of the heel of the hand for a few moments, either in the bowl or on a floured surface.

At this stage you can shape the dough and put into tins, or set it aside to rise in an oiled bowl inside a large polythene bag. If you have time this does not need to be in a very warm place and long risen dough has a better texture. It can take several hours, but in the end should be doubled in bulk. When stretch marks begin to appear the rising is going too far, and the dough should be punched down.

Cut into pieces for each tin. Knead some more, smooth into shapes and set to rise in the tins. They rise well if they are enclosed in big polythene bags, but again warmth is not so important unless you need to get them baked for a certain time.

When well risen loaves should be baked in a pre-heated oven at 230°C/450°F (Gas Mark 8) for 20 minutes and then reduce heat to 200°C/400°F (Gas Mark 6) for a further 20 to 30 minutes depending on the place in the oven and the size of the loaves. When bread is cooked it should come easily from the tin and have a hollow sound when knocked. Another test is to 'listen' to the loaf. If it has stopped 'singing' (i.e. if you hear nothing!) it is cooked. But if you hear a sound inside the loaf put it back in the oven for a few more minutes.

In any case it is a good idea if you like crusty loaves to return the loaf upside down for a few moments to brown all over. Cool the bread as quickly as possible and freeze the next day. For details and tips about freezing see page 11.

Variations

There are so many variations possible on this basic loaf. You can vary the flours by using rye and barley flours in different quantities; but remember that they do not contain so much gluten as wheat and so the result will be heavier – but tasty and nutritious! Some people like to add a quantity of 81 per cent or even unbleached white flour for a lighter loaf, and these may be better when making sweet breads.

Delicious loaves can be made by adding grated nuts, sunflower or sesame seeds, sprouted seeds, malt and a little molasses. Soya flour can be added in greater quantity or left out altogether. I like to add a little for extra protein.

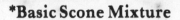

*Basic Scone Mixture

225g (8 oz) plain wholewheat flour
50g (2 oz) at most, soft vegetarian fat
150ml (¼ pt) milk – this can be cow's milk or soya
milk or yogurt. It is best if the milk is sour – a little
lemon juice will help to do this
2 to 3 level teaspoonsful baking powder (less if sour
milk)
1 level teaspoonful cream of tartar
1 tablespoonful golden syrup
pinch of salt

Mix all the dry ingredients and sieve them. Rub in the fat
with a light 'high' movement to get as much air into the
mixture as possible. Add syrup, rubbing that in too. Pour
in most of the liquid, mixing with a knife, only adding
last drop if needed. It should be a soft spongy dough.

Knead very lightly and either form into two balls
which are then flattened and cut across to form triangles
or roll out and cut into shapes.

Put onto a greased baking sheet, and leave for about 15
minutes before putting into the top of a hot oven,
230°C/450°F (Gas Mark 7) for about ten minutes.

The scones can be glazed with milk or egg or dusted
with flour.

To freeze: These scones freeze very well. Wait until they
are cold then put into a polythene bag.

Storage life: 3 months.

To thaw: Thaw at room temperature for about an hour
or straight into a warm oven for ten minutes.

*Treacle Scones

As above but add treacle instead of syrup and about two tablespoonsful of dark brown sugar. Make sure the scones are really soft before baking.

*Currant Scones

As above but add about a handful of currants and a little soft brown sugar.

*Cherry Scones

As above, adding a few halved cherries and a little soft brown sugar.

*Herb Scones

Rub in a tablespoonful yeast extract with the fat, and add two tablespoonsful fresh minced herbs.

Cheese Scones

Omit the syrup, add 50g (2 oz) finely grated cheese with the dry ingredients. The addition of an egg to all these scones will improve the texture and they can all be frozen in the same way as the basic scone.

Biscuits

225g (8 oz) plain flour
100g (4 oz) margarine
75g (3 oz) soft brown sugar
yolk of 1 egg

Mix the flour and sugar, rub in the fat and add the egg. The mixture should be softer than a pastry mixture. This is basic – now by dividing it into three you can make three different biscuits. Here are some suggested flavours:

Vanilla – use sugar in which a vanilla pod has stood for some weeks.

Coconut – add two tablespoonsful of dessicated coconut, and work into the mixture.

Chocolate – work in 25g (1 oz) grated plain chocolate.

Orange – work in a tablespoonful of grated orange peel.

Form each third into a long roll after kneading for a few minutes to obtain a smooth consistency. Wrap each roll separately in film and then foil and put straight into the freezer. The rolls can be shaped to give different sections, e.g triangular, square, round. They can also be rolled into smaller sizes and then joined together in a long strip to make variegated biscuits.

Freeze for at least an hour before cutting very thinly and baking on greased baking trays in an oven 170°C/325°F (Gas Mark 3) for 10 to 15 minutes.

These biscuits can be left in their rolls in the freezer for up to three months. Take out and cut while still frozen. This gives lovely thin crispy biscuits.

*Shortbread

Proportions for shortbread are:

6 of flour
4 of butter or margarine
2 of sugar

The flours can be mixed and one part of soya flour substituted. Just mix all ingredients together to form a firm dough. This goes through a 'breadcrumb' stage when it seems that it will not come right, but just knead the pieces together and they will cohere.

Press into a shortbread mould or roll out and cut into fingers. A mould should be dusted with sugar and then the shortbread can easily be released on to a greased baking sheet. Prick neatly over or score with a fork. Bake in oven at 170°C/325°F (Gas Mark 3) for about ¾ hours.

To freeze: Cool completely and freeze.

Storage time: 3 to 4 months.

To thaw: Thaw at room temperature for about an hour.

Cherry Shortbread

Add a few glacé cherries chopped up.

Currant Shortbread

Sprinkle a little demerara sugar on top and a few currants before baking.

Apricot Spiced Honey Cake

175g (6 oz) 100 per cent flour
100g (4 oz) soft margarine
175g (6 oz) clear honey
75g (3 oz) dried apricots – soaked for 1-2 hours
2 teaspoonsful mixed spice
2 teaspoonsful baking powder
3 tablespoonsful milk
1 large egg

Sieve flour, mixed spice and baking powder. Then add all the other ingredients, except apricots, and beat to a smooth consistency. Chop the apricots into small pieces and fork them into the mixture. Bake in a greased loaf tin at oven 180°C/350°F (Gas Mark 4) for 45 to 50 minutes.

Very tasty when cold with slices spread with a little butter.

To freeze: Cool and freeze whole cake, or cut into slices and open freeze before wrapping. Latter way means you can use a few slices at a time.

Storage life: 3 months.

To thaw: Stand at room temperature for two to three hours.

Wholemeal Swiss Roll

**50g (2 oz) 100 per cent flour weighed after the bran
has been sifted out
50g (2 oz) soft brown sugar – put through a sieve
(white castor sugar will give a lighter finish)
2 eggs**

Filling:
jam or jam and cream, or butter icing or fruit

Preheat the oven at 220°C/425°F (Gas Mark 7). Line and grease an 11 ins x 7½ ins baking tray.

Sift the sugar on to a piece of foil on a plate and put it in the oven for three minutes on a low shelf, then break the eggs into a bowl, add the sugar and whisk until the mixture is really light in colour and doubled in bulk – best to use an electric mixer. Fold in the flour very gently and spread into the lined tin. Make sure the corners are well covered. Bake on the top shelf for eight minutes. The cake should be just retracted from the edges and spring back when gently pushed down.

Dredge a thick sheet of paper with sugar and turn the cake out on this. Wet the edges of the paper lining the cake with a finger and peel it off.

Immediately trim all the edges of the cake and then roll it up. It can then be gently unrolled when cool and filled. Alternatively, spread with jam and then roll. A variety of soft fruit can be spread over, either on its own or with cream or a butter cream.

To freeze: Allow to cool and then open freeze and pack.

Storage life: 2 months.

To thaw: Stand at room temperature for one to two hours.

The same recipe can be used for a sponge sandwich, putting the mixture into two greased and lined sandwich tins. If the mixture is a little thicker they will take a few more minutes to cook.

15
SWEET DISHES

Apple Fritters

**Firm sweet apples
50g (2 oz) 100 per cent flour
12g ($\frac{1}{2}$ oz) soya flour
5 tablespoonsful tepid water
1 egg white
pinch of salt
2 teaspoonsful olive oil or similar**

Mix flours, salt, oil and water to a smooth batter that will coat the back of a spoon. While deep fat is heating core and slice apples to $\frac{1}{2}$-inch thickness. Whisk egg white stiff and fold with metal spoon into batter mixture. Coat apple rings and drop into fat, cook until crisp and golden. Remove and drain on absorbent paper. (Shallow fat can be used when fritters will need to be turned.) Serve with a little soft brown sugar.

To freeze: Pack with film or foil between layers.

Storage life: 2 to 3 months.

To thaw: Preheat in hot fat or put straight in to hot oven for about 20 minutes.

Baked Alaska

1 baked sponge cake
Ice-cream
100g (4 oz) soft brown sugar, light
whites of 2 eggs

The sponge cake can either be a round half cake or half an oblong swiss roll. (See recipe page 125)

Take the ice-cream from the freezer and pile a mound in the centre of the sponge, leaving at least half an inch all round. Return to the freezer.

Beat the egg whites until they are stiff. Make sure that the sugar is fine and not lumpy (I put mine in an electric coffee grinder and then sieve it). Add the sugar gradually by tablespoonsful, whisking each time. The meringue must remain firm and hold a peak. If by some mischance it does not do so you will have to abandon the pudding or start again.

Bring the ice cream out of the freezer and completely cover it with meringue so that it is properly sealed in. Bake in a very hot oven 230°C/450°F (Gas Mark 8) for three minutes. Slip onto a cold serving dish and serve at once.

This pudding will not freeze as such, but the sponge and ice-cream will come out of the freezer. It is also possible to put the whole Alaska into the freezer with the meringue in position for a short time. For instance if you prepare it immediately before serving the first course it can go into the freezer until you are ready to put it into the oven.

Baked Apples with Fruit

**4 good cooking apples
2 tablespoonsful each, raisins, chopped dates,
chopped dried apricots
juice of half a lemon
2 tablespoonsful honey
cinnamon, nutmeg**

Put honey and lemon juice into a small saucepan and simmer for a moment adding a little cinnamon and grate of nutmeg. Then soak the fruit in this mixture while preparing the apples.

Wash the apples and take out cores to be sure no coarse parts are left. Run a sharp knife round middle of skins. Put the apples in an oven dish and press fillings in. Pour three tablespoonsful of water into dish. Bake at 200°C/400°F (Gas Mark 6) until ready. Do not overcook. Serve as they are with cream, nut cream or custard.

To freeze: Cool pack into rigid container (separating each apple with film or foil), label and freeze.

Storage life: 2 to 3 months.

To thaw: Bring out four hours before needed to eat cold. To eat hot put frozen apples into oven at 180°C/350°F (Gas Mark 4) for about 30 minutes (cover tops with foil to prevent burning).

Debbie's Delight

2 cupsful breadcrumbs
50g (2 oz) brown sugar
50g (2 oz) margarine
¼ cupful chopped dates
½ cupful sliced and toasted almonds
½ cupful dried apricots, soaked overnight and
drained and chopped small
½ cupful prunes, soaked overnight, just brought to
boil, cooled, drained and chopped
1 apple, sweet or good cooking, chopped fine
thick whipped cream or thick yogurt
a little rum or liqueur

Melt margarine in a saucepan, add the sugar, and stir over gentle heat for about five minutes then add breadcrumbs, toss for a few more minutes, allow to cool then add all the ingredients leaving cream until the last. Put into a dish and put into freezer for at least twelve hours. Remove from freezer and keep at room temperature for two to three hours before eating.

This can be stored in the freezer for a month. Evaporated milk could be used instead of cream. Chill before whipping. Whip really stiff and add a little sugar if liked.

*Fruit Crumble *(enough for 2 crumbles)*

About 1kg (just over 2 lbs) cooking apples with any other fruit mixed in. For example, add any of the following fruits from your freezer: blackcurrants, blackberries, red currants, raspberries, strawberries. Just throw in a small handful after the apple is cooked; it is surprising how the taste comes through, making this an economical way of improving on plain apples.

For the crumble:
100g (4 oz) 100 per cent flour
225g (8 oz) oat flakes
25g (1 oz) soya flour
50g (2 oz) ground almonds
175g (6 oz) margarine
175g (6 oz) dark brown sugar

Mix all the ingredients together and rub in the fat to resemble breadcrumbs.

Put the fruit into a freezer proof container and cover evenly with the crumble mixture. Cook in oven at 200°C/400°F (Gas Mark 6) for 45 minutes.

Method 1
To freeze: Allow to cool, cover, label and freeze.

Storage life: 2 to 3 months.

To thaw: Leave for four hours in room temperature to eat cold.

Method 2
To freeze: Freeze uncooked.

Storage life: 2 to 3 months.

To thaw: Put straight into a heated oven, allow extra 15 minutes cooking time.

Method 3

To freeze: Just freeze the crumble mixture in a labelled polythene bag.

Storage life: 2 to 3 months.

To thaw: Use crumble mixture on fruit.

Variation

For plain apple crumble add mixed spices to crumble mixture.

*Danish Girl with Veil

About ½kg of cooking apples (just over 1 lb) cooked to a *purée* with 4 cloves and a piece of bruised root ginger.

**50g (2 oz) butter or margarine
75g (3 oz) dark brown sugar
175g (6 oz) brown breadcrumbs
3 or 4 gingernuts, crushed**

Melt fat in a large saucepan, add sugar and stir so as not to burn for two to three minutes, then gradually add crumbs and crushed ginger nuts. Stir to absorb moisture and crisp crumbs.

Take off heat. Fill freezer proof see-through dish with alternate layers ending with crumbs. (It looks nice if the last layer of apple has a ring of crumbs round the outside.) Serve chilled with thickly grated dark chocolate round the edge. Eat with cream, or nut cream (see page 155).

To freeze: Seal dish in polythene bag when cool, label and freeze.

Storage life: 2 to 3 months.

To thaw: Leave for four hours in room temperature or in fridge overnight. Decorate before serving.

Variation
To make this dish extra special, while crumb mixture is still warm pour on a little chocolate liqueur, brandy or rum and stir.

Ice-cream

410g (14¼ oz) tin evaporated milk
1 egg
75g (3 oz) soft brown sugar that has been in a jar with
a vanilla stick

Put the can of milk into the fridge for some hours before using (or not more than half an hour in the freezer). Have all ingredients as cold as possible. Make sure that the sugar is as fine as possible – this can be done by putting it through an electric coffee grinder. Whisk the milk until it is really stiff. An electric mixer is ideal for this. Gradually whisk in the sugar once the milk is as stiff as possible. Beat the egg a little and add.

Transfer immediately to a large oblong container and put into the coldest part of the freezer as you want it to freeze as quickly as possible.

There is often a lot of fuss made about making ice-cream and this is the most simple way. The mixture may settle a little but on the whole retains its texture very well. It can be stored for several months. Bring out about 15 minutes before needed.

Variations

This ice-cream can form the basis of all sorts of variations; here are a few suggestions.

Chocolate. Melt some block chocolate in a dish set in a pan of hot (not boiling) water. When the ice cream mixture is quite ready swirl in the melted chocolate, then freeze quickly. A little liqueur is a very tasty addition to this.

Rum and raisin. Snip a few raisins in half using scissors and soak for a few hours in some rum. Drain and add to the ice cream just before freezing.

Fruit ice-cream. The addition of all sorts of fruits makes this ice-cream really delicious. They need to be chopped small and whipped into the mixture just before freezing. Be sure not to leave large pieces of fruit or they will be too frozen to enjoy when the ice-cream is ready to eat. Raspberry and strawberry turn a lovely pink.

A Lighter Ice-cream

The ingredients are just the same as the basic ice-cream, except that the egg yolk is not used. Whip the egg white separately and incorporate it with the milk and sugar as before. This tends to hold its shape even better in the freezer.

It should be noted that freezing tends to reduce the flavour of ice-creams and so it is necessary to be sure that they are extra well flavoured. Sugar helps to bring out the flavour, but too much sugar retards the freezing process.

Water ices are very refreshing and can be made simply by combining strong fruit juices with some sweetener.

Although a light brown sugar can be used there is no doubt that this has a taste and so white sugar allows the fruit taste to be more true. Honey has the same disadvantages as brown sugar.

Raspberry Ring

Chou pastry (see page 43)
Slightly sweetened whipped cream
Raspberries

Prepare a baking sheet by first greasing it lightly and then dust with flour. Lay a suitable plate on top and trace with the back of a spoon around it. Remove the plate.

Make the choux pastry and spoon the mixture round the circle that you have traced leaving a hole in the centre.

Bake in a hot oven 220°C/424°F (Gas Mark 6 for about 20 minutes or until the pastry is firm. Remove, cool a little and then carefully cut the pastry ring in half. Take out any uncooked dough. Line the bottom with raspberries pile whipped cream on top, replace the lid and put more raspberries in the centre.

To freeze: The ring can be frozen like this for a few days, but it is better to freeze without cream. Put carefully into a container.

Storage life: 2 months.

To thaw: Put frozen unwrapped ring in a very slow oven for about 15 minutes, cool and then fill.

If using frozen raspberries they should be thawed for about two hours before using.

This is delicious if the raspberries (or some of them) are marinaded in some liqueur, such as kirsch, for about an hour. Use these to fill the centre and use the dry raspberries for the ring itself.

Spicy Cheese and Apple Flan

75g (3 oz) 100 per cent flour
25g (1 oz) oatflakes
25g (1 oz) millet flakes
25g (1 oz) soya flour
75g (3 oz) dark brown sugar
75g (3 oz) margarine
100g (4 oz) cheshire cheese, grated
3 good sized cooking apples, chopped fine
2 teaspoonsful mixed spice
2 teaspoonsful cinnamon
pinch cardamom
25g (1 oz) almonds, grated
50g (2 oz) raisins
clear honey

Rub mixture into mixed flours and flakes, add the sugar and mix well. Press into an 20cm (8 in) flan tin, making sure it goes well up the sides.

Mix spices, apples, raisins and nuts together. Layer them with the cheese into the flan case. Then dribble a generous measure of honey on top. Bake at 200°C/400°F (Gas Mark 6) for 30 minutes.

To freeze: Open freeze when cold. Keep in the tin and wrap. This is because flan tends to crumble.

Storage life: 3 months.

To thaw: Thaw at room temperature for about three hours. Can be eaten cold or heated.

16
QUICK MEALS FROM THE FREEZER

Inevitably there are times when you have to produce a meal in a very short time. This is where the freezer will be invaluable. There follow a variety of recipes that will take no more than half an hour to prepare from the beginning, and this assumes in some cases that you will also be putting on potatoes or rice to cook or making a simple salad. These recipes also assume that you are making good use of your freezer and that it is well stocked.

If you always keep a stock of burgers of various kinds and some basic sauce roux or béchamel you will have no problems about producing a variety of quick meals.

A few uncooked pie shells and some prepared pastry mixture will ensure that you can make an interesting savoury or sweet. *Purées* take a long time to thaw and so cannot be used quickly for a pie, but soft fruit can be put straight into a dish to be cooked.

Remember to put the oven on straight away if you are going to need it, and always use large shallow dishes for quick cooking. If you are suddenly called on to produce a meal without warning here is a suggestion.

*Quick to Prepare Menu

**Nutburgers, using nut savoury mixture (page 87)
already shaped into burgers and frozen ready to fry
Potatoes
Peas
Grated carrot
Quick tomato sauce
Fruit crumble with cream or a quick custard**

First light the oven, then take the ready mixed pastry crumbs out of the freezer and some soft fruit such as strawberries, raspberries, gooseberries, redcurrants.

Put about 5 tablespoonsful of the mix in a bowl add about 2 tablespoonsful of dark brown sugar and mix. Put the fruit into an oven dish and add one chopped cooking apple if you have one handy. Cover with the crumble and put into the oven at 190°C/375°F (Gas Mark 5).

Now do the potatoes. Cut them small and put to cook with a little mint from the freezer. Take the burgers and roux, two tomatoes and a cube of tomato *purée* out of the freezer.

Heat oil in the frying pan and while it is heating start preparing the carrots. Put burgers on to cook, and, in the meantime, finish grating carrots. Pop tomatoes in with potatoes for 30 seconds, remove with draining spoon and you can then peel off the skin.

Heat some water. Put roux in liquidizer with tomatoes, salt and pepper, tomato *purée* and some basil and parsley or similar herbs. Add a little water and liquidize, using just enough water to make smooth mixture. Transfer that to a pan and stir over heat. By this time you will be ready to pop some peas in hot water (with mint) to cook.

Burgers should now be ready and on a serving dish, potatoes drained and sauce just about bubbling. The peas will only take a moment or two. So you are ready to serve up a simple but appetizing meal. By the time you have eaten the first course the crumble will be cooked.

This is a sample of the sort of thing that can be accomplished. The following recipes give basic ideas and you can decide which vegetables to add.

*Cashew Cauli with Mushroom Sauce

frozen cauliflower
frozen roux or béchamel sauce base
frozen mushrooms
small onion, frozen
a little milk or water
salt and pepper
nutmeg
dash paprika
50g (2 oz) cashew nuts, chopped

Remove all ingredients from freezer. Heat milk or water. Put roux, mushrooms, chopped onion, salt and pepper, grate of nutmeg, dash paprika into liquidizer, add just a little water and liquidize until blended.

Transfer to a saucepan and heat, stirring until it thickens. Meantime, cook cauliflower in very little water. If there is any water left after cooking cauliflower this can be used to add to sauce. Chop cashews and toast under grill. Put the cooked cauliflower into a shallow dish, pour sauce over and then sprinkle nuts on top. Put under grill to finish off.

Mixed Vegetable Drops

25g (1 oz) 100 per cent flour
1 dessertspoonful soya flour
150ml (¼ pt) milk
1 egg
salt and pepper
4 tablespoonsful mixed diced vegetables from
freezer
1 tablespoonful peas
1 tablespoonful sweet corn
oil

Take all the vegetables from the freezer and spread out on a large plate to thaw. Sift flours and seasoning together, drop egg in centre of flours in a bowl, add a little milk and beat flour into liquid, adding more milk as needed. Add all the vegetables. Then drop in spoonfuls into hot shallow fat. Cook both sides.

Serve with potatoes or a good brown rice.

Mushroom Drops

Ingredients as for batter in mixed vegetable drops.
225g (8 oz) mushrooms from the freezer

Drop the mushrooms straight into shallow fat, and cook quickly both sides. Drain and then proceed as for mixed vegetable drops.

Onion Drops

Recipe exactly as for mushroom drops. If onion has already been fried and frozen it can be put straight into the batter. If frozen uncooked then put into shallow fat from frozen and fry for about five minutes.

Savoury Pancakes

Pancakes are an obvious choice for a quick meal. They can be filled with any variety of tasty things. Below several suggestions are given for fillings.

Mushroom Mixture
100g (4 oz) mushrooms
1 onion
2 tomatoes
grated nuts
salt and pepper, basil
tomato ketchup

Bring the pancakes out of the freezer and put them on a plate over a saucepan of simmering water.

Rough chop the mushrooms, tomatoes and onion, put a little oil in a pan and add these ingredients with a crushed clove of garlic, if liked. Shake and simmer with a tight lid for about ten minutes. During this time you can prepare a simple salad.

Stir the vegetables, add seasoning and ketchup, stir in the nuts, leaving a few back. Fill pancakes, roll them up and put into a dish suitable for grilling for a final heating. Sprinkle the rest of the nuts on top.

Cottage Cheese and Nuts
225g (8 oz) cottage cheese
50g (2 oz) nuts, chopped
1 small onion or chives, chopped and marinated in a
little vinaigrette for ten minutes if possible
salt and pepper
chopped mint or thyme

Toast the nuts under the grill, having put the pancakes to heat on a plate over a saucepan of boiling water. Put the cheese, onion herbs and some salt and pepper into a pan and very gently heat, stirring and adding the nuts. Fill pancakes and finish heating under grill.

Grated Hard Cheese and Chopped Apple

Simply take the grated cheese out of the freezer, and spread it out to thaw quickly. Chop a cooking apple fairly finely. If liked crush some garlic and mix this with either the apple, some made mustard, a handful of fresh chopped herbs or a few herbs crumbled from the freezer.

Heat the pancakes over water on a flat plate. Either sprinkle the cheese mixture on the pancakes that are heating, or gently heat under grill or in a pan. The object is simply to ensure that the cheese is completely thawed and not to cook it.

Roll the pancakes up with cheese mixture in and then put under the grill with a sprinkling of cheese on top to finally heat the whole dish.

Good with a green vegetable and new potatoes, or with a salad.

Curry Pancakes
1 cooking apple
1 Onion
raisins
clove garlic
parsley (which can be from the freezer)
curry sauce (see page 110)

Put the pancakes to thaw and heat. Chop the apple and onion. Put these in a pan with a little oil and *sauté*. Add garlic if liked when onion is cooked then add the sauce, raisins and parsley, heat through and then fill the pancakes and finally heat under grill if it seems necessary.

Spinach Flan

**One uncooked pie case, frozen
spinach, frozen
4 eggs
salt and pepper**

Light the oven. Return uncooked pie case to its original ring or dish and put straight into oven at 200°C/400°F (Gas Mark 6) for ten minutes.

Meanwhile, cook the spinach in a slight amount of water, checking that it is not burning and breaking it up as it thaws.

Beat the eggs together adding salt and pepper. When spinach is quite thawed chop it up and make sure there is not too much liquid, although there can be a little. Add eggs to spinach and stir round over low heat to begin cooking. Then take pie case out of oven and pour spinach mixture into it. Sprinkle a little cheese on top (or some breadcrumbs) and return to the oven lowering heat to 180°C/350°F (Gas Mark 4). It will be ready in about ten minutes.

Sweetcorn Batter Pie

Pastry mixed to 'breadcrumb' stage
Sweetcorn, frozen in kernels
Mushrooms
Onion rings

Batter:
25g (1 oz) 100 per cent flour
1 dessertspoonful soya flour
150ml (¼ pt) milk
1 egg
salt and pepper
1 tablespoonful mint, chopped

Light oven at 220°C/425°F (Gas Mark 7). Use enough pastry mix to line a pie dish. Do not make into pastry just add the chopped mint to the 'crumbs' and a little salt and pepper and press down at the bottom of the dish.

Make the batter and add to it a good quantity of mushrooms and sweet corn from frozen. Scatter some onion rings on the bottom of the pie and then add the batter mixture. Cook in oven as set for half an hour.

Quantities will depend on size of dish, but if the meal is needed in a hurry choose a large shallow dish.

Serve with salad.

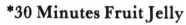

*30 Minutes Fruit Jelly

For this jelly you can use a shop bought vegetarian jelly which only has to have boiling water poured on and stirred vigorously.

575ml (1 pt) fresh fruit juice or half water and half fruit juice
2 tablespoonsful honey or soft brown sugar
2 level teaspoonsful agar agar

Take a quarter of the fruit juice or half the water and sprinkle in agar agar, whisking. Put this over the heat and continue whisking until it almost reaches boiling point. Make sure all the agar is dissolved, then take off the heat, and stir in the rest of the liquid and the sugar or honey. Stir well, put into a shallow dish which is rather larger than may appear necessary. Add from the freezer a handful of frozen raspberries, loganberries or strawberries. Stir these in and the coldness of the fruit will quickly cool down the jelly.

Although you should not put warm things in a refrigerator I make this an exception if I am really in a hurry for a sweet. By the time you have eaten your first course the jelly will be sufficiently set to serve.

17
ENTERTAINING
WITH YOUR FREEZER

One of the first things the new freezer owner has to learn when entertaining is to keep quiet about the new acquisition.

This is not because there is anything shameful about owning a freezer – far from it – but when guests compliment the hostess on her food, and she blurts out that it has all been in the freezer for the last three months there is likely to be a noticeable relinquishing of knives and forks among non-freezer owners. They simply do not understand how well a freezer keeps food, their only experience probably being badly cooked 'mush' in a restaurant.

Incidentally when, preferably afterwards, they learn that some of the food came out of the freezer there is often a quick conversion to the ranks of freezer owners.

Another thing to remember is to jot down the ingredients on the label when you freeze food that is going to be eaten by guests. This may seem an odd suggestion, but I have been caught out a few times when asked for the recipe! Of course I ought to know exactly what is in it, but like most people who enjoy cooking I have probably added a few things that were not in the original recipe and I simply cannot remember precisely. It is a complete give-away that you have not been slaving away that day to prepare the meal!

Party Food

Party food should be delicate, tasty and attractive. People who are accustomed to using 100 per cent flour in bread, pastry and cakes; whole grains; dark brown sugar and lots of raw salads, need to make concessions when entertaining guests who are unused to these things. Taste is mainly dictated by habit and there is no point in offering food so unfamiliar that your guests will not enjoy it.

My usual solution is to grind my own wheat, but sieve out the bran and mix the flour with some unbleached white flour, this lightens the whole thing, but still gives some of the delicious taste of freshly ground wheat.

Many of the recipes in this book will do very well at any occasion, ranging from a simple pizza party to a formally decorated savoury nut roast for a dinner party. There are many suggestions on the sandwich pages that will be suitable for children's parties, and picnics. The cheese flans will be very good cold for packed lunches and so will picnic pies and the pasties in the vegetable section.

With carefully chosen accompaniments, good sauces and some simple decorations your guests will certainly not miss the meat course.

There follow some ideas for simplifying the decorations, and a few recipes for tasty snacks. Garnishes for soups will be found in the section on soup.

Easy Decorating

One of the pleasures of party food is the attractive display. Yet those final decorative touches can take up an awful lot of time.

The actual decorating usually needs to be done on the day of the party, but with a freezer most of the decorative 'bits and pieces' can be prepared days in advance. For instance you can slice stuffed olives thinly, cut red pepper in regular shapes such as strips, diamonds, triangles, squares, petal shapes etc., turn gherkins into flowers then simply put them into a container in the freezer several days in advance.

Carrots are colourful for decoration. Use a tiny aspic cutter, push it as far as it will go into a raw carrot, remove and then thinly slice the carrot, and you have a number of identical shapes.

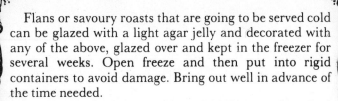

Flans or savoury roasts that are going to be served cold can be glazed with a light agar jelly and decorated with any of the above, glazed over and kept in the freezer for several weeks. Open freeze and then put into rigid containers to avoid damage. Bring out well in advance of the time needed.

A quick way of decorating a cold flan is with piped cream cheese. This too can be put in the freezer ready piped. Little cream cheese rosettes topped with olive, sweet corn or other savoury decoration can be stored ready for immediate use. For sweet dishes prepare rosettes of cream or butter cream.

Quick effective decorations are pastry shapes. Make these from pieces of puff or short pastry 'over' at odd times. They can be triangles, ovals, circles, etc. They should be glazed and baked, then frozen in boxes. Use directly out of the freezer on savoury flans. Either lay overlapping all round or stand up by piping a spot of cream cheese in which to anchor the shape, and set them round in a symmetrical pattern.

*Agar Glaze

Agar agar is a seaweed jelling agent and is obtainable at most wholefood stores. It is expensive, but only a little is needed at a time. Agar sets very quickly indeed.

Use a level teaspoonful of agar to 275ml ($\frac{1}{2}$ pt) of water. Whisk the agar into the cold water and bring to the boil. You can add a little yeast extract if you want to colour the glaze, but usually decorations that are brightly coloured, such as red pepper and sweet corn, look better with a clear glaze.

Boregi Brehan

Short crust pastry made with 100 per cent flour with bran sieved out, or 81 per cent flour

Filling 1
1 small onion, chopped
½ red pepper, chopped
1 tomato, skinned and chopped
oil, salt and pepper
1 tablespoonful of chopped parsley
1 teaspoonful of paprika

Sauté the onion and pepper in a little oil for five minutes, add the rest of the ingredients and mix well, stir over heat for a few minutes and then put aside.

Filling 2
1 large egg, hard boiled and chopped
50g (2 oz) cottage cheese
2 tablespoonsful of finely chopped chives
salt and pepper, large pinch cayenne

Mix all together and beat smooth. Set aside.

Filling 3
Butter beans that have been cooked with a sprig of rosemary, seasoned with salt and pepper and 1 dessertspoonful of made mustard, mashed into one egg. Set aside.

Roll out the pastry very thinly. Cut into 2-inch squares. Brush with butter or oil. Using different fillings put about a tablespoonful of filling down the centre (or just off centre). Roll into a cigar shape. Brush with egg and put onto a greased baking sheet. Bake in oven 190°C/375°F (Gas Mark 5) for about 15 minutes until golden and crisp. Serve hot or cold.

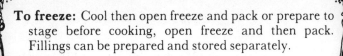

To freeze: Cool then open freeze and pack or prepare to stage before cooking, open freeze and then pack. Fillings can be prepared and stored separately.

Storage life: 2 months.

To thaw: Thaw overnight in fridge and bring into room temperature two hours before serving cold or put straight into oven and allow extra time to serve hot. Brush with egg after freezing.

Noisettes Nemrod

100g (4 oz) cashew nuts, finely ground
100g (4 oz) hard cheddar cheese, finely grated
1 very small onion or chives, finely chopped
1 tablespoonful parsley, minced
½ teaspoonful dry mustard or 1 teaspoonful made mustard
salt and pepper (if needed)

Mix all together well and knead to make sure it adheres. Shape into small finger shapes, egg and crumb, or brush over with oil. Fry in shallow fat or bake on oiled tin in hot oven. Baste and turn after ten minutes and cook for a further ten minutes.

Method 1

To freeze: Cool the cooked noisettes and freeze on a flat freezer plate, separating layers with film or foil.

Storage life: 3 months.

To thaw: Heat frozen noisettes in hot fat until heated right through or heat in oven.

Method 2

To freeze: Freeze uncooked shaped noisettes.

Storage life: 3 months.

To thaw: Egg and crumb and cook as above.

18
SANDWICHES

It is very convenient to be able to make a batch of sandwiches at one time. However, they will deteriorate if left more than about six weeks, so care must be taken to label and rotate stock.

Some rules for freezing sandwiches:

1. Cut bread fairly thinly.
2. Many books recommend cutting off crusts, but this really seems a shame.
3. Be sure bread is fresh and not dry or heavy.
4. Cover right to edges with butter or margarine.
5. Make really tasty fillings.
6. DO NOT USE: sliced tomatoes, lettuce, sliced hard boiled egg, mayonnaise. Instead serve lettuce and quarter tomatoes and half hard boiled eggs separately, unfrozen.
7. Tomatoes can be mashed in with other ingredients, and well mashed or scrambled eggs can be used.
8. Open freeze sandwiches on trays then wrap and label. Thaw by unwrapping and covering with a cloth.
9. Thaw in refrigerator overnight or at room temperature for 2-4 hours, depending on filling and warmth of room.

Below are a few ideas for sandwich fillings and savoury butters.

*Aubergine Spread

**450g (1 lb) aubergines, in thick slices
1 large onion, chopped fine
3 tablespoonful lemon juice
1 clove garlic, crushed
1 big leaf fresh basil minced or ½ teaspoonful dried
basil or oregano
2 large ripe tomatoes, skinned and chopped
salt and pepper
1 tablespoonful tahini
oil**

Sauté aubergine and onion in oil until soft but not 'mushy' and add garlic in the last couple of minutes. Put all ingredients into a liquidizer and blend together. Test for taste and adjust.

Use on sandwiches or, as a first course, on a bed of lettuce. Do not freeze for more than two weeks. The spread can be frozen in a container on its own. Thaw at room temperature or in the refrigerator.

*Avocado and Almond Filling

**1 large avocado, mashed with 1 dessertspoonful
lemon juice
50g (2 oz) almonds, finely ground
2 drops tabasco
salt and pepper**

Mix all together, seasoning to taste. Vary this filling by using different kinds of nuts.

Cottage Cheese Fillings

Cottage or cream cheeses make a basis for many interesting fillings. Try a variety of the following: chopped chives; crushed pineapple; mashed tomato with oregano and fresh black pepper; chopped olives and gherkins; chopped toasted nuts; chopped mint; onion rings; chutneys; blue cheese. Every variety of herb can also be used roughly chopped together and various weeds such as chick-weed, ground elder and dandelion. Dandelion is rather bitter and should be used very sparingly.

You can sprinkle on these fillings various seeds such as sunflower seeds, chopped nasturtium seeds and so on. You can also use sprouted seeds for sandwiches. They can be frozen, but will lose some of their nutritional value. (See page 158)

*Rolled-up Sandwiches

To make sandwiches 'special' you can roll them in a swiss roll fashion. You need soft, even, textured bread and the crusts must be cut off.

Spread filling generously, then cut part way through bread in a straight line ¼ in from edge to be rolled inside. This helps the roll to start. Skewer each roll with a cocktail stick, freeze, then take out sticks and wrap. When thawing sandwich rolls should maintain their shape.

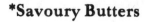

*Savoury Butters

Savoury butters are another handy 'extra' to keep in the freezer. Make them and then divide to freeze in small quantities. Thin squares thaw more quickly. Open freeze on a tray and then pack in rigid containers, separating layers with foil or film.

To use, put straight on cooked vegetables or allow half an hour to thaw for sandwiches or decorative piping. For all the following use either butter, margarine, soya or other nut fats. You can make your own nut fat by grinding the nuts to an emulsion in a coffee grinder – any nuts can be used, brazils being the most fatty.

Chive Butter. Chop very finely, add a little black pepper and blend into butter.

Curry Butter. Sauté one small chopped onion in a little butter, then add a teaspoonful of curry powder, good pinch garam masala and a ¼ teaspoonful of curry paste. Stir all the time until the onion is soft. Allow to cool, put through a fine sieve and then blend into butter. Only keep for two to three weeks in freezer.

Garlic Butter. Add crushed garlic to butter according to taste, include a little parsley if liked. Only keep for two to three weeks in freezer.

Mint Butter. There are many mints from which to choose: peppermint, pineapple, spearmint, applemint. Check that they suit your personal taste first – applemint is sure to please. Put the washed and dried mint with a few sprigs of parsley through a herb mill, then blend with butter and mix well.

Mustard Butter. Make a thick mustard and when it has stood for about ten minutes beat into the butter.

Paprika. Add about ¼ teaspoonful to 25g (1 oz) butter.

Parsley. Chop well or put through parsley mill and blend.

Thyme. As parsley.

Watercress. Make sure watercress is well cleaned and dried, then chop very finely or put through a parsley mill.

It is obvious that the variety of savoury butters is almost endless, bounded only by your ingenuity and freezer space.

19
FRESH RAW FOODS

This short chapter is included as a 'reminder' that no one should eat out of a freezer all the time, and that to be really healthy we all need a good proportion of raw, fresh foods each day.

Just about all the vegetables that are normally eaten cooked can also be eaten raw; the exception being potatoes.

The secret in making fresh, raw food attractive is certainly in the preparation. It may be that a carrot is better for you if the only preparation is that it is cleaned, and the teeth do the rest, but for most people this is taking healthy living a bit far, and they would prefer some of the 'chewing' work to be done by kitchen graters.

Nevertheless in order to preserve as much goodness as possible it is better to grate coarsely rather than finely. Leave the cutting of fruit and vegetables until the last minute, and put on a light dressing to seal the cut surfaces and stop the vitamins and minerals from leaching out. The simplest dressing is lemon juice, which will also help preserve a good colour.

Vinaigrette

Another easy dressing is a vinaigrette. Take a $\frac{1}{4}$ teaspoonful each of salt, pepper and mustard and beat them into 1 tablespoonful of lemon juice. Stir in about 150ml ($\frac{1}{4}$ pt) olive oil (or other vegetable oil) and add any variety of herbs, such as thyme, tarragon or mint. A small clove of garlic can be cut and added, or you can rub cut garlic round the plate or dish before mixing the salad.

Such a vinaigrette will keep for many weeks. Cider vinegar can be used instead of lemon juice. To avoid a

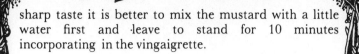

sharp taste it is better to mix the mustard with a little
water first and leave to stand for 10 minutes
incorporating in the vingaigrette.

Accompaniments

Raw foods make good accompaniments to hot dishes, and
they can either be served on a side plate or with the hot
meal. Hot and spicy food, such as curry or Mexican dishes
go particularly well with a salad of sliced tomatoes, grated
carrot and crisp lettuce. Medium grated or chopped white
cabbage marinated for an hour or so in a herb vinaigrette
with a few raisins and some chopped apple is good with
lentil dishes or nut roasts.

Chop some florettes of cauliflower finely, add grated
brussel sprouts and sliced raw mushroom with some
sliced onion and marinate in vinaigrette for an hour or
two, then eat as a filling to a hot pancake or
accompaniment to cheese drops.

Grated beetroot is tasty if mixed with a little lemon
juice and yogurt and a grate of nutmeg. As well as going
well with a mixed salad it can be used as a separate
vegetable to hot dishes.

If raw foods are not part of the main meal it is a good
idea to make a small salad as a start to the meal. Fruits
can also be used in this way. Grapefruit and melon are
the norm, but there is no reason why grated apples,
sliced oranges or pears sharpened with a little lemon
juice, should not be used.

Obviously a fresh fruit salad to end a meal is ideal.
The freezer can help you add a touch of luxury by the
addition of raspberries or strawberries out of season.
Raspberries are excellent eaten raw from the freezer, but
strawberries should not be allowed to thaw completely or
they become too soft.

Sproutings

Several recipes mention sprouted seeds, beans or pulses.
Although one can buy large sprouted mung beans
(chinese beans) they are in fact usually well past their
best for eating. You can make your own sproutings with

very little trouble, small expense and in a tiny space.

All you need, basically, are several large, clean jam jars and some thin pieces of cloth or muslin to cover them and, of course, the seeds, beans or pulses. The tremendous urge for life which is in all living things will quickly do the rest. As soon as you introduce dry seeds to water they react. Sproutings are just the germinated seeds bursting with the vitamins and essential minerals that would normally turn them into a full grown plant. The best time to use them is after they have been growing for four days – a little longer perhaps for some larger beans.

The amount that you start at one time will depend on your needs, and the size of the seeds. If you have not grown sproutings before you will be very surprised at how much can be made from so little.

Take about a tablespoonful of seeds. Cover them with warm water in a jar, put a cloth over the top to keep it clean, and then set the jar in a warm place, such as an airing cupboard overnight. Next morning remove the cloth, put your fingers over the top of the jar and let all the water trickle out.

From then on all you have to do is make sure that your seeds are moist. Do not leave any water in the jar, but from time to time gently cover the seeds with water, and then trickle it out again. If you leave the jar in your airing cupboard, the seeds will grow more quickly, but you are more likely to forget them. It is a better idea to keep them in sight in the kitchen. If there is ever any sign of fermentation wash right through thoroughly several times, and the sproutings will probably be all right. If you let them go too far in fermenting throw them out and start again.

You can sprout almost any whole seed, bean or pulse. For example: alfafa, chick peas, beans of all sorts, lentils, fenugreek, soya beans, wheat, oats, barley and rice. If the seeds grow on after the four days they are still quite alright to eat but are not so rich in vitamins. Sproutings can be frozen, but obviously they will lose some nutrition and it is better to eat them fresh. If, occasionally you do wish to freeze sproutings there is no need to blanche but do not keep in the freezer for long.

RECIPE INDEX

Agar Glaze, 148
Apple Fritters, 126
Apple Savoury, 57
Apricot Spiced Honey Cake, 124
Asparagus Ravioli, 103
Aubergine Bake, 45
Aubergine Spread, 153
Avocado and Almond Filling, 153

Baked Alaska, 127
Baked Apple with Fruit, 128
Basic Béchamel, 108
Basic Loaf Recipe, 118
Basic Roux, 107
Basic Scone Mixture, 120
Basic Sweet Dough, 115
Béchamel, Basic, 108
Bohemian Cabbage, 56
Boregi Brehan, 149
Borsch, 113
Brazil Nut and Pilaf, 93
Bubble Tea Bread, 116
Buns
   Chelsea, 116
   Thumb, 117
Butter Bean Croquettes, 80
Butter Bean Timbale, 75

Cannelloni in Cheese Sauce, 105
Caper Sauce, 109
Cashew Cauli with
   Mushroom Sauce, 139
Casserole of Onions with
   Brazils and Cashew Nuts, 58
Casserole of Vegetables with
   Soya Protein, 68
Cauliflower Casserole, 69
Celeriac Potato Boats, 46
Chelsea Buns, 116
Cheese and Onion Flan, 49
Cheese and Potato Bake, 44
Cheese and Tomato Flan, 49
Cheese Flan, 47
Cheese Pie, Mushroom and Cream, 52
Cheese Pudding, 48
   variations of, 48
Cheese Sauce, 109

Cheese Scones, 121
Cheese Soufflé, Quick, 53
Cheesey Hazelnut Roll, 50
Cherry Scones, 121
Cherry Shortbread, 123
Chunky Almond Pie, 70
Cider Savoury, 71
Cottage Cheese Fillings, 154
Currant Scones, 121
Currant Shortbread, 123
Curry Pancakes, 142

Danish Girl with Veil, 132
Debbie's Delight, 129
Dough, Basic Sweet, 115

Fried Bean Croquettes, 76
Fruit Crumble, 130

Garnishes, 112

Hazelnut and Cashew Savoury, 86
Hazelnut Balls
   in Curry Sauce, 85
Hazel Nut Roll, Cheesey, 50
Hazel Wheat Roll, 84
Herb Scones, 121

Ice-cream, 133

Lentil Bake, 78
Loaf Recipe, Basic, 118

Mexican Beans, 79
Mushroom Wholegrain Flan, 94
Mushroom and Cream Cheese Pie, 152
Mushroom Cheese Drops, 51
Mushroom Drops, 140

Noisettes Nemrod, 151
Nut and Paté Ravioli, 104
Nut Savoury Mix, 87

Onion Drops, 140
Onion Flan with Artichokes
   and Tomato, 59

Onion Sauce, 110

Pancakes, 100
Pancake Pudding, 99
Paprika Pilaf, 93
Parsley Sauce, 109
Pastry
cheese, 42
chou, 43
for flan cases, 40
herb, 42
rough puff, 41
savoury, 42
short crust, 40
Pea Pod Soup, 114
Picnic Pies, 60
Pizza, 99
Potato Surprise, 61

Quick Curry Sauce, 110

Raspberry Ring, 135
Red Cabbage Roll with
Nut Stuffing, 62
Rice and Walnut Gratin, 92
Roux, Basic, 107
Russian Nutburgers, 89

Sandwiches, Rolled-up, 154
Sauce
caper, 109
cheese, 109
onion, 110
parsley, 109
quick curry, 110
tomato, 111
Savoury Pancakes, 141
Savoury Butters, 155
Savoury Whole Grain Flan, 96

Scones
cheese, 121
cherry, 121
currant, 121
herb, 121
treacle, 121
Scone Mixture, Basic, 120
Scotch Eggs, 54
Shortbread, 123
cherry, 123
currant, 123
Soup, 112
pea pod, 114
Soya Bean Stew, 81
Spicy Cheese and Apple Flan, 136
Spinach Flan, 143
Spinach Ravioli, 102
Split Pea Burgers, 77
Stuffed Lasagne, 105
Stuffed Peppers, 98
Sweet and Sour Carrots, 64
Sweet and Sour Nut Burgers, 90
Sweetcorn Batter Pie, 144
Swiss Roll, Wholemeal, 125

Thirty Minutes Fruit Jelly, 145
Thumb Buns, 117
Tomato Sauce, 111
Treacle Field Beans, 82
Treacle Scones, 121
Vegetable Pasties, 65
Vegetarian Moussaka, 91
Vegetarian Sausage and
Egg Plate Pie, 55
Village Pie, 72
Vinaigrette, 156

Wholemeal Swiss Roll, 125

Yeast Tea Ring, 117